21st
Century
Gorshkov

TITLES IN THE SERIES

21ST CENTURY FOUNDATIONS

Benjamin Armstrong, *editor*

In 1911 Capt. Alfred Thayer Mahan wrote in his book *Armaments and Arbitration*, "The study of military history lies at the foundation of all sound military conclusions and practices." One hundred years later, as we sail ever further into the twenty-first century, we are commonly told we face the most challenging circumstances in history, or that it is more dangerous now than ever before. These exaggerations tend to ignore the lessons of strategy and policy that come from our past.

The 21st Century Foundations series gives modern perspective to the great strategists and military philosophers of the past, placing their writings, principles, and theories within modern discussions and debates. Whether drawn from famous men or more obscure contributors with lesser known works, collecting and analyzing their writing will inform a new generation of students, military professionals, and policy makers alike. The essays and papers collected in this series are not provided in order to spell out cut and dry answers or exact procedures, but instead to help make sure we ask the right questions as we face the challenges of the future. The series informs the present by collecting and offering strategists and thinkers of the past.

21st Century Gorshkov

The Challenge of Sea Power in the Modern Era

Edited by Kevin Rowlands

Naval Institute Press

Annapolis, Maryland

This book has been brought to publication with the generous assistance of Marguerite and Gerry Lenfest.

Naval Institute Press
291 Wood Road
Annapolis, MD 21402

Library of Congress Cataloging-in-Publication Data is available.
ISBN: 978-1-68247-159-3 (paperback)
ISBN: 978-1-68247-160-9 (ebook)

♾ Print editions meet the requirements of ANSI/NISO z39.48-1992 (Permanence of Paper).
Printed in the United States of America.

25 24 23 22 21 20 19 18 17   9 8 7 6 5 4 3 2 1
First printing

CONTENTS

ACKNOWLEDGMENTS

This is an edited volume and so my first debt of gratitude must go to someone I have never met and never will—the author, Sergei Georgiyevich Gorshkov. Without him this book, quite obviously, could never exist. Of course, Gorshkov wrote in Russian and published most of his material in the Soviet Union; little of it was translated for publication in English. However, the navies of the West were interested in what Gorshkov had to say during the height of the Cold War and I am grateful to Stephen Prince and Jock Gardner of the Royal Navy Historical Branch for allowing me into their archives to find contemporary translations of Gorshkov's articles.

The Western navies did not hold the copyright, however, and I am very pleased that the management of *Morskoy Sbornik*, the Soviet/Russian Naval Digest in which the majority of Gorshkov's works appeared, granted permission to reprint his writing with appropriate acknowledgment. Again, my lack of Russian precluded any direct liaison but Lieutenant Commander Ryan Coatalen-Hodgson, the assistant naval attaché at the British Embassy in Moscow, acted as a brilliant go-between.

BJ Armstrong, the series editor and brain behind the simple but effective idea of bringing classic but too often forgotten naval thought to the attention of a new generation of readers, helped enormously and, annoyingly, was always right with his suggestions. I'm proud to say that he has become a good friend. Glenn Griffith, acquisitions editor at the Naval Institute Press, kept me on the straight and narrow, and I am similarly grateful to the whole staff at NIP who were not only willing to run with the idea, but who turned the idea into a smart-looking book. And thanks go to my copy editor Wendy Bolton, who has the eyes of a hawk and patience of a saint!

Finally, my biggest thanks go to my wife Emma and daughter Maya, who after five years of watching me work for a PhD simply took in their stride the fact that I wanted to read and write about a long-dead Russian sailor. It is to them that this book is dedicated.

INTRODUCTION

When Admiral of the Fleet of the Soviet Union Sergei Gorshkov retired from active service in 1985 he had been commander in chief of the Soviet navy for almost three decades. In that time he completely changed his service and made it the most powerful maritime force that Russia ever possessed. It was a remarkable achievement and gave his country unprecedented influence far beyond its shores. Now, a century after the Russian Revolution and almost three decades after the collapse of the Soviet Union, an event that led to a period in which the combined fleets of the West were unchallenged in their command of the seas, there is renewed interest in the history of the Cold War. The time is right for new, objective assessments of the confrontation that shaped most of the second half of the twentieth century, not only for theoretical or academic reasons but also for practical implications. Russia is resurgent on the world stage; China and India are turning their attention to the maritime domain. Equal measures of instability and opportunity abound in Africa, South America, the Middle East, and Asia. In an increasingly globalized, interconnected world, now is not the time for isolationism—anywhere.

A naval planner, sitting in one of the capitals of East or South Asia in the second decade of this century, wondering how to shape his or her country's involvement with the sea, is faced with a choice of two historical models. States starting from a relatively low baseline but harboring significant maritime ambitions could take their lead from those that have long exercised sea power and continue to do so. But the barriers to entry on these terms are great. The costs can be prohibitive and, even if they could be afforded financially, there would inevitably be a shortfall in skill, experience, societal engagement, and, perhaps, political mind-set. Where to begin? When building maritime power from scratch, only the unwise would start with a nuclear-powered aircraft carrier.

An alternative for those planners could be to challenge the status quo in a different way, adopting some lessons from a man who was the architect of the biggest and most rapid naval expansion program in peacetime history. Under Gorshkov's leadership, the Soviet navy was transformed from a small, backward, coastal defense force into an oceangoing, blue-water giant. Consequently, the Union of Soviet Socialist Republics (USSR) was transformed from being a continental power with little or no interest in the sea, a power that viewed navies as optional extras, into a global maritime player able to challenge the West at the height of the Cold War. It is no mean feat to change the outlook and culture of a whole nation in such a way; it takes vision, organizational ability, and staying power.

It is fair to say that naval theory and policy have long been swayed by Western thought. Over centuries what amounts to an Anglo-American school of sea power has dominated strategy and practice; the Royal Navy and U.S. Navy, either alone or acting together with allies, have effectively ruled the waves as global naval hegemons for over three hundred years. This simple fact is arguably the result of geography. Because Great Britain is an island and because the United States is protected by enormous oceanic distances, those countries have been largely immune to land invasion. As a result their characters have developed to reflect their maritime interests and they have become outward facing; their trading endeavors led to economic supremacy, and their navies evolved to become agents of power and influence, the guardians of vital choke points and the defenders of sea-lanes of communication. It is a story that has been told well by Alfred Thayer Mahan, Sir Julian Corbett, and other prophets of sea power.

Gorshkov knew this when he took over the helm of the Red Navy. He would later explain that if the Soviet Union had followed exactly the Western pattern of naval development it would have found itself in the position of a relative novice competing against experienced, old hands. By taking advantage of the revolution in military affairs, as it applied at the time to his navy, and adopting such things as nuclear propulsion, missile technology, and electronic sensor and weapon systems, they could leapfrog stages of development and compete as equals.[1]

There is always an alternative approach. Over a century ago the French *Jeune Ecole*, for example, advocated quantity, speed, deception, and the use of novel technology such as the torpedo and novel tactics such as hit and run. It was a direct attempt to face up to the dominance of the

Royal Navy without embarking on a crippling, tit-for-tat arms race. Similarly, between the two world wars the Soviet Union had its own *Young School*. Russia had always been a land power and after the 1918 revolution the new Bolshevik government focused its efforts on building up the Red Army; it was not immediately concerned with naval development.[2] Typical of the Soviet leadership's view of the extravagance of having a powerful navy are the words of Boris Shaposhnikov, chief of staff of the Red Army between 1928 and 1931: "To our misfortune, the maritime costs devilish sums of money, and therefore its development should strongly answer to the necessity of meeting the objectives that could fall on to it. Luxuries should not be permitted."[3]

This dismissiveness, however, gave Soviet naval modernizers scope to try something different. They concentrated on submarines. By the late 1930s the Red Navy had little surface capability to match the most modern European, American, and Japanese battleships, but it did possess the largest underwater fleet in the world and was fast becoming a force to be reckoned with. It does not take much of an intellectual leap to see a version of that simple but effective offset strategy repeated today in Chinese or Iranian anti-access/area-denial (A2AD) technologies and tactics.

However, alternative approaches that are driven by necessity, as the Young School's were, tend to fade when their proponents later find that they can afford to replace them with the "real thing." The Soviet Young School's model was never formally endorsed by Stalin and from the mid-1930s onward, when communism still held the promise of economic success, measures were taken to start to build a bigger, more traditional fleet that could symbolize Soviet power and prestige; it was the fleet that ultimately would see action in World War II. That fleet contained many of the elements that the U.S. Navy, Royal Navy, and German Kriegsmarine held dear, but it was not an exact replica. The utility of sea power was not intuitively understood in Moscow. To get to the next stage of development the Red Navy needed a champion.

The War Hero

Sergei Georgiyevich Gorshkov was born in 1910 at Kamianets-Podilskyi, in what is now western Ukraine, but grew up in Kolomna near Moscow. It was a troubled region, then as now, and after Gorshkov's World War I childhood and the Russian Revolution, Bolshevik rule would have brought some semblance of stability.

At the age of seventeen Sergei Gorshkov decided where his future lay and he joined the Frunze Naval School in Leningrad, keen to make a career for himself in the navy. He spent four years at Frunze, the leading naval academy in the USSR, before graduating in 1931 and returning to Ukraine. He spent the bulk of his service before reaching high rank as an officer in the Black Sea Fleet. He progressed quickly in the 1930s; his talent was spotted and he was commanding small ships just a year after leaving the academy. He completed the destroyer commanders' courses locally in 1937, aged just twenty-seven, and attended advanced senior commanders' courses in 1941, just as Nazi Germany was launching Operation *Barbarossa*. As what the Russians call the Great Patriotic War started, Gorshkov already had had commands of escort ships, a destroyer, a destroyer squadron, and a cruiser squadron under his belt.[4] He was ready to fight.

Gorshkov's war record was as impressive as his peacetime advancement. He distinguished himself commanding the Azov and Danube Flotillas, seeing action throughout 1944 and taking a leading naval role in the liberation of the Balkans from Nazi rule. His war experiences would stay with him and form a significant part of his writing in later years. After the war, in 1948, he became the chief of staff of the Black Sea Fleet and its commander in 1951 when he was still just forty-one years of age. Admiral Kuznetsov, then the commander in chief of the Soviet navy knew talent when he saw it and appointed Gorshkov his first deputy in June 1955; six months later Kuznetsov had fallen from favor and suddenly Gorshkov was in charge.

The Patient Politician

No one stays at the top of their profession, overcoming all challenges and challengers, for thirty years without an innate ability for political maneuvering. Whether this maneuvering is around small "p" office politics or big "P" affairs of state is almost irrelevant to the longevity of the individual; only the consequences and perhaps the manner of their departure differ. A key quality required to maintain such senior positions is an ability to understand the times, to sense the political "weather" and to work with it rather than battle against its relentless headwinds. There are few places in history more unforgiving to those who got it wrong than the upper echelons of the leadership of the USSR; from Lenin and Stalin, Khrushchev and Brezhnev, to Gorbachev and the final fall of communism, the Kremlin was awash with plotting, intrigue, infighting, backstabbing, and more than the occasional palace coup.

Admiral of the Fleet of the Soviet Union Sergei Gorshkov, commander in chief of the Soviet navy, deputy minister of defense, Hero of the Soviet Union, was in his element in that environment from the mid-1950s until the mid-1980s, serving under five premiers. As others fell by the wayside he had staying power and steadily took the navy from being a poor relation to the other armed services to the front rank of strategic importance. He was certainly a sailor and a leader, but he was also a politician. He had to be. When cuts had to be made, he made them. When there were opportunities for growth, he took them.

The journey he led the Red Navy on was one of incremental progression but it is probable that one moment in time accelerated the process. The Cuban Missile Crisis of 1962 was a humiliation for the Soviet Union and a particular embarrassment for its navy. The predominantly submarine fleet had proven impotent in the face of the American quarantine of Cuba. Khrushchev had no desire to repeat the experience and reportedly summoned Gorshkov to tell him so. Gorshkov, seizing his chance, reassured his leader that a new shipbuilding program would deliver the USSR a modern, balanced fleet able to project its power over the world's oceans and end Western maritime supremacy.[5] All he then had to do was deliver it. Some people make the political weather, others ride it.

The Architect

It would be wrong to think that Gorshkov built the Soviet navy from scratch during his tenure at the top. A mix of capabilities existed before he became commander in chief, but he sought to bring greater coherence and balance to the fleet that he inherited: balance between mission types, between classes of ship, between people, and between its global dispositions.

Gorshkov the architect knew that his design must start with the right foundations. The Soviet navy had long been criticized as a force that developed some high-end platforms but lacked the infrastructure to make optimum use of them. The physical geography that had made Great Britain and the United States leading sea powers worked to constrain the Soviet Union in its attempt to break out of the mold of being solely a continental power. The four fleets of the Red Navy faced enormous challenges that Gorshkov had to navigate before he could ever get them to be able to operate in what he termed the "World Ocean."

First, the Northern Fleet bases were closed by ice for six months of the year and the Baltic and Pacific Fleets were similarly affected for about three months each winter. In the late 1950s the USSR had just a handful of diesel-powered icebreakers in service, but the pace of development ramped up significantly under Gorshkov. The world's first nuclear-powered surface ship, the icebreaker *Lenin* became operational in 1959, and over twenty new diesel icebreakers were built and entered service during the 1960s, allowing the navy to reach the high seas year-round and, importantly for Gorshkov's wider concept of sea power, providing more regular access to the Northern Sea Route along the Russian arctic coast from the Kara Sea to the Bering Strait. Then, from the early 1970s the *Arktika*-class nuclear icebreakers, the most powerful ever built, began to enter service and gave the Soviet Union an assured path to the sea.

Second, even during ice-free periods, each of the fleets was constrained by having to pass through choke points the West would find relatively easy to dominate. The Northern Fleet had to break through the Greenland-Iceland–United Kingdom (GIUK) gap if it were to reach the Atlantic; the Baltic Fleet needed to pass through the Kattegat and Skaggerak; the Black Sea Fleet was confined by the Turkish Straits before it could reach the Mediterranean; and the Pacific Fleet was hindered by the La Perouse Strait to the north of the Japanese Home Islands and by the Tsushima Strait between Japan and South Korea.

To break through each of these choke points, to achieve local sea control, would take a dedicated effort. Making it possible to pass through the GIUK gap, for instance, became a substantial role for the Northern Fleet submarine force, particularly the diesel boats designated by NATO as the *Foxtrot* class and the first- and second-generation nuclear boats of the *November* and *Victor* classes. To a certain extent long-range aviation aircraft such as the *Bear*, *Backfire*, and *Badger* bombers also had a role to play in clearing the way for the striking force ships that would follow on.

The narrow seas affecting the Baltic, Black, and Pacific Fleets were less suitable for submarine operations and, here, Gorshkov fell back on his amphibious experience in World War II. The Soviet naval infantry had effectively been disbanded in 1947, its remnants incorporated into coastal defense forces, but it was revived by Gorshkov in the 1960s and became better enabled by the addition of transport ships and landing craft to the fleet. Never an expeditionary invasion force, in the manner of the U.S. Marine Corps in World War II and later, the naval infantry was developed for limited area operations including the seizing and holding of strategically important straits to allow the free passage of the fleets that they served.[6]

Once in the World Ocean, the Soviet fleets faced another major problem—sustainment. Gorshkov was acutely aware that his navy did not have a tradition of replenishment at sea or a network of logistic bases around the globe. The Soviets would never completely overcome the sustainability constraint but Gorshkov worked to fix it by introducing auxiliary supply ships, by conditioning his sailors to longer periods away from home ports, and by negotiating support facilities with friendly and aligned states. At various times Albania, Cuba, Angola, South Yemen, Syria, and Vietnam all proved vital to the Soviet forward presence.

That forward presence was maintained by an increasingly capable and numerically large mix of platforms that could deter, strike, and influence. The USSR operated conventionally powered ballistic missile submarines from the mid-1950s, but following the success of the nuclear-powered icebreakers Gorshkov brought nuclear-powered, nuclear missile–carrying boats (SSBNs) into service. The *Hotel* class was followed by the *Yankees* and *Deltas* and then by the *Typhoons*. By the end of Gorshkov's career the USSR had one and a half times as many SSBNs as the U.S. Navy, though their numbers of warheads and their yield was significantly less. Nonetheless, the submarine remained the capital ship of the Red Navy and in addition to the strategic bombers there were large numbers of attack submarines tasked with anti-ship, particularly anti-carrier, missions.

The Soviet navy's own aircraft carrier development program was less successful, but ships were built. In the late 1960s the *Moskva*-class aircraft-carrying, anti-submarine cruisers were introduced, and in the 1970s the *Kiev* class came into service with vertical takeoff and landing aircraft; their role was to strike both land and maritime targets. Finally, the *Tbilisi* class (with the lead ship named *Admiral Kuznetsov*) joined the fleet in the mid-1980s. However, the main striking capability of the surface fleet was provided by a series of cruisers. The *Kynda*, *Kresta*, *Slava*, *Kirov*, and *Kara* classes, for example, included nuclear-powered vessels capable of speeds of over thirty knots, carrying anti-aircraft and anti-ship missiles with huge ranges of up to two hundred miles.

Of course, such platforms were worthless without suitably qualified and experienced sailors to man them. Much of Gorshkov's writing in the articles and passages that follow recognizes this and focuses on the human element of naval development. Never exactly the socialist utopia of Marx's aspirations, the Soviet system that Gorshkov was dealing with was hindered by a stark difference between officers and enlisted personnel. Officers, generally, were intelligent, well-educated professional volunteers, trained for their jobs, competent and politically aware. In contrast, the enlisted sailors tended to be conscripts from the various outlying regions of the USSR, poorly educated, the recipients of very limited basic training and low pay. Consequently, whereas officers could make a career at sea (as Gorshkov had done), enlisted sailors invariably left at the end of their three-year draft; this resulted in a chronic shortage of the senior non-commissioned personnel required in a modern, technically advanced navy.[7] Navies still wrestle with this problem today. How are valuable technicians retained when higher pay, home, family, and stability beckon?

The Strategist

Far from simply being a successful naval administrator able to maneuver within Soviet politics, Sergei Gorshkov was a skilled proponent of grand strategy. Perhaps more straightforward to achieve in a single-party state operating a command economy, he was able to make the intellectual and practical links between national interest and the day-to-day employment of the armed services. Taking a full spectrum approach decades before it was fashionable, before the West even began to debate "joint," "cooperative," and "whole-of-government" operations, Gorshkov drew together the exploitation of natural resources, the conduct of mercantile business, the enabling legal frameworks, societal needs, politics, and maritime security into his vision of sea power. He was an advocate of deterrence, as were the majority of his Cold War contemporaries, but he also emphasized the importance of the littoral and of environmental protection. He was ahead of his time. He saw clearly that by combining the various elements of sea power, which included not only the navy but also fishing fleets, the merchant marine, and scientific research, the state could progress: "It is reasonable to consider that the totality of the means of harnessing the World Ocean and the means of defending the interests of the state when rationally combined constitute the sea power of the state, which determines the capacity of a particular country to use the military-economic possibilities of the ocean for its own purposes."[8]

It should be remembered that Gorshkov took command of the Soviet navy at a time when most strategists, in both the Eastern and Western blocs, assumed that any future war between the major powers would quickly become nuclear. The USSR saw its principal threat not in NATO's conventional ground or sea forces, but in a surprise first-strike attack by the U.S. Strategic Air Command. In such a war it was assumed that there would be minimal naval participation; consequently, little effort was expended in beefing up the role of the Red Navy. Before Gorshkov, and in the immediate aftermath of World War II, Western freedom of maneuver on the global commons was, if not liked in the East, then certainly taken for granted.[9]

Gorshkov, however, was a student of naval history, patriotic, and a keen watcher of the West. As Western thinkers debated naval diplomacy, discussing themes from coercion to cooperation, his opinions were also forming. He used his knowledge of Western maritime strategy to introduce a forward-presence mission to a fleet that had traditionally concentrated on local defense and support of the army. Importantly, he intuitively understood that the navy was extremely useful in operations other than war and could confer prestige on its owner: "The strength of the fleets was one of the factors helping states to move into the category of great powers. Moreover, history shows that states not possessing naval forces were unable for a long time to occupy the position of a great power."[10]

What is also apparent, however, is that his vision was largely reactive. He saw NATO as "an alliance of maritime states, with powerful naval forces occupying advantageous strategic positions in the World Ocean." The true intention of Western sea power in peacetime, he wrote, was "gun diplomacy."[11] Gorshkov used the term "local wars of imperialism" to describe his interpretation of Western strategy and offered the opinion that naval forces were the most versatile and useful instruments of state military power because of their mobility, persistence, independence, and their ability to be deployed or withdrawn at will. The attributes are clearly recognizable to twenty-first-century eyes and though Gorshkov used them in his analysis of NATO strategy they were universal and equally applicable to his own forces. His "local wars of imperialism" label was obviously a politically charged term but the sense is familiar.

Gorshkov's genius was not simply to grow his navy, it was to justify its existence as an arm of the state in peacetime and in operations that fell short of all-out war. His notion of furthering national interest through forward presence was not always adversary-centered. In addition to the coercive potential of naval forces he saw a central role of sea power as a means of "holding in check" allies to manage or maintain power relationships. The Soviet Union may have been the most powerful country in the Warsaw Pact, but its leverage over satellite states, other countries within its sphere of influence, and the Third World varied wildly. He was particularly intrigued by the British-American relationship and thought it "interesting" that the United States achieved its position of relative maritime pre-eminence in the twentieth century through close partnership with the UK, a position Germany had failed to reach through confrontation.[12]

Emphasizing the soft power potential of the Red Navy, Gorshkov built up a fleet that not only comprised a credible fighting force, but one that deployed to nontraditional operating areas with a forthright agenda to extend communist influence through ambassadorial deployments. One of the most famous passages from *The Sea Power of the State* amply demonstrates his thoughts:

> The Soviet navy is also used in foreign policy measure by our state. But the aims of this use radically differ from those of the imperialist powers. The Soviet navy is an instrument for a peace-loving policy and friendship of the peoples, for a policy of cutting short the aggressive endeavors of imperialism, restraining military adventurism and decisively countering threats to the safety of the peoples from the imperialist powers. Soviet naval seamen . . . feel themselves ambassadors for our country. Friendly visits by Soviet seamen offer the opportunity to the peoples of the countries visited to see for themselves the creativity of socialist principles in our country, the genuine parity of the peoples of the Soviet

Union and their high cultural level. In our ships they see the achievements of Soviet science, technology and industry.[13]

The Writer

Luckily for today's readers, Gorshkov was not only an exceptional organizer, skillful politician, and insightful strategist, he also committed himself to paper. As a writer he is perhaps best known in the West for two pieces of work that appeared in the 1970s. First, he exposed his thoughts in a series of articles, originally published in the Soviet journal *Morskoy Sbornik* (Naval Digest) in 1972–73, which were translated and reproduced in the U.S. Naval Institute *Proceedings* magazine throughout 1974. The *Proceedings* articles, which ran to eleven in total and were published in consecutive issues from January to November of that year, were each accompanied by a commentary by a prominent U.S. Navy flag officer, including such luminaries as Arleigh Burke and Stansfield Turner. The column inches that the American publication gave to the Russian's thoughts over almost an entire year, and the degree of parallel analysis, is recognition of the importance of his writing to the geopolitical situation of the time. As Rear Admiral Miller, USN, wrote following the first installment: "His writings should be studied as assiduously as European statesmen studied Alfred Thayer Mahan's works during the years preceding World War I. They are of considerable importance in determining the nature and scope of the big-power competition to be expected in the years to come."[14]

The "Gorshkov articles," as they were colloquially known, were officially titled "Navies in War and Peace" and offered a combination of historical analysis, contemporary Soviet naval thinking, and, it must be said, communist propaganda. They were put together and published in book form in English under the title *Red Star Rising at Sea*. What is clear from Gorshkov's work is that it was written primarily for a domestic Russian audience. Indeed, one commentator wrote in a critique that three major objectives were apparent: Gorshkov was attempting to justify the importance of a navy to great power status, he was enlisting Communist Party support for the Navy, and he was explaining his theory to Soviet sailors.[15]

Nonetheless, the success of the articles in both East and West led to a more detailed exposition of Gorshkov's thinking with the appearance of his most celebrated book, *The Sea Power of the State*, published first in Russian in 1976 and then in English in 1979, again through the Naval Institute Press. The central tenet of *The Sea Power of the State*, and of the preceding articles, was the direct correlation between great power status and great navies. However, time and again he also made clear that a *military* navy is not enough. A military navy is but one arm of a successful sea power and needs to be accompanied by suitably scaled maritime economic might.

The anthology of Gorshkov's works in this book includes some of his most famous writing—it would be a lesser volume if it did not. The first and last of the "Navies in War and Peace" articles are included, as is a substantial passage from *The Sea Power of the State*. They offer a taster; readers wanting more from Gorshkov should turn to those sources. Together, they reveal the man at his most eloquent, describing the importance of historical analysis, explaining why the USSR needed a navy, and delving deep into one perspective on the components of sea power.

The remainder of the selected texts, however, is a more raw collection of Gorshkov's writing for *Morskoy Sbornik* that has not previously been published widely in English. In these the reader may see a subtly different commander in chief, at times gushing with enthusiasm for communism and the Soviet state, at others frustrated by the lethargy and inadequacy of his navy, and always cognizant of the relative advantages enjoyed by NATO. They can be exasperating in their language, particularly in the opening sections, with their attacks on the West and uncompromising, over-the-top rhetoric in praise of Party and State. Objective they are not. However, readers will be rewarded by persevering through the propaganda to the kernel of the message each time.

So why should we read Gorshkov? We should read him because he offers us more than we are used to. We have become accustomed to accepting the wisdom of the West, of Mahan and Corbett, without question simply because we "won." Those strategists should not be discarded, but no one should believe that naval thought reached its pinnacle in the first decades of the twentieth century and can never be improved. Gorshkov gives us an alternative lens through which to view alliances, civil-military relationships, technology, diplomacy, and leadership. But it is not just us. The doctrines of the rising maritime powers in Asia bear more than a passing resemblance to Gorshkov's. After all, if you were one of those planners in China or India trying to build a navy for the modern era, where would you start? Perhaps with the man who did it.

CHAPTER ONE

Teamwork

L ike the majority of his generation, Sergei Gorshkov's character was shaped in large part by war. By the summer of 1944 Europe was all but torn apart. The amphibious and airborne landings in Normandy hit Nazi Germany from the West, the Italian Campaign continued to pressure the Axis powers' southern "soft underbelly" and, in the East, the juggernaut of the Red Army marched relentlessly toward Berlin. Against this backdrop the thirty-four-year-old Gorshkov, already a rear admiral, was given command of the Danube Flotilla, a formation within the Soviet Black Sea Fleet.

To achieve such rank and to be entrusted with such responsibility at so young an age is a measure of both the times and the man. Gorshkov's own account of his command is therefore a good introduction to him as an individual. It wasn't high command, it was subordinate. It wasn't a purely naval endeavor, it was joint. He wasn't the supported commander, he was supporting. What the young Gorshkov had to do, and what comes across in his article "Soviet Seamen in the Battles to Liberate the Danube States," was to work as part of a team to achieve a greater good than he, or they, could have realized by working alone.

Interestingly, the timing of the publication of the article in *Morskoy Sbornik* also says something about its author. Gorshkov had risen to become commander in chief of the Soviet navy under Nikita Khrushchev's premiership and had, it was rumored, been a key figure in the removal of Marshal Georgii Zhukov as minister of defense in 1957. Zhukov, a hero of the

Soviet Union and perhaps *the* Soviet military figure of World War II, was a declining star in the mid- to late 1950s and never a keen navalist. By 1964 when the article was published Khrushchev himself was on precarious ground and it was becoming apparent that his days were numbered. Gorshkov would have been aware of the discontent in and around the Kremlin and his own future was by no means certain. Retelling his story of the war, in parts in great detail and always thoroughly researched (the names of commanders and key personalities, for instance, are never missed), reminded his Soviet readers that the head of their navy was not merely a hero and senior officer, but also a modest man and a team player. By the end of the year Khrushchev was ousted, yet Gorshkov remained for another two decades. The article didn't save him, but it does provide insight into his veracity and the strength of his bureaucratic and political skills.

Gorshkov earned his place in the history of what the Russians call the Great Patriotic War. His flotilla was undoubtedly a force multiplier, but his story is recounted here in a relatively minor supporting role, working at the behest of more powerful—principally army—commanders. He had to form agile, cooperative relationships with national and international counterparts. He was consistently professional, reliable, and trusted.

The Danube Flotilla was in essence a riverine squadron whose mission was to penetrate inland, seizing ports and transporting men and matériel as they went, all the while clearing mines and providing gunfire support to the troops onshore. It was an essential component within that favorite obsession of Soviet commanders—operational art. The ability to place tactics in the context of strategy across an entire front is easily articulated but incredibly difficult to deliver, yet it was mastered by the Soviets in eastern Europe in 1944. Gorshkov explains how submarines and torpedo cutters struck Nazi sea lines of communication, how simultaneous air strikes hit shore targets in Romania and enemy fleet units, and how the preeminent ground forces progressed to their objectives. The selection of targets and sequencing of activity worked well and one might presume that each tactical commander instinctively knew his place in the plan. Gorshkov certainly knew his role and makes clear that alongside his responsibility for the Danube Flotilla, he was also naval deputy to the 46th Army commander.

Teamwork in war can take many forms. Gorshkov noted that within the flotilla itself particular attention was paid to the preparations for operations, including a "vast indoctrination program among the seamen." The language of indoctrination may seem out of step with today's less politically motivated but more politically correct approach to training, but the sentiment is sound. Gorshkov's men, and they were all men, were made aware of the importance of their cause and their responsibility as individuals to work together to achieve it.

Intra- and interservice cooperation leaps from the page with Gorshkov's words. His experience in the hard-fought, rolling amphibious campaign convinced him that victory in war is rarely the gift of one service alone. The land, maritime, and air forces of the USSR at least had the opportunity to prepare together and work to a common plan. What is perhaps more remarkable in this history was the ability of the Soviet armed forces to rapidly integrate Romanian, Bulgarian, and Yugoslav elements, some regular but many irregular forces, as momentum built on their westward advance. The Red Army and Navy were seen by many in those countries as liberators and acted as a catalyst for revolution. The strategic significance of fighting alongside peoples who only days before had been under Nazi rule far outweighed any tactical difficulties of language, culture, tactics, techniques, and procedures. The point was not lost on the future commander in chief.

In the twenty-first century we in the West are often quick to talk the language of cooperation, of joint operations, and integrated, whole-of-government approaches, but do we really understand what that means? Sergei Gorshkov gives examples of how it was done in his time and the core lessons are equally applicable in ours. We might balk at the thought of "indoctrinating" our sailors, but we should not shy away from ensuring that they know what they are fighting for: national and international security. We might claim to be "joint," but how many times have we prioritized purely naval outputs over those that contribute to other services or overall defense objectives? We might seek international "partnerships" and "coalitions," but are our systems and methods compatible, or have we priced ourselves out of the market? Working as a team does not mean getting others to join our bandwagon. It means, at times, subordinating ourselves to the needs of others and compromising on some of our own aims safe in the knowledge that we are working toward the greater good. Gorshkov knew this and the underlying sense in the author's words is that it was the people, working together as a team with a common goal, who really mattered.

SOVIET SEAMEN IN THE BATTLES TO LIBERATE THE DANUBE STATES

Morskoy Sbornik, 1964

This year will mark twenty years since the Danube River states were liberated from the Hitlerite invaders by Soviet forces and international anti-fascist forces. The Danube countries were occupied by Hitlerite Germany during World War II. Some of them—Rumania, Hungary, and Bulgaria—were drawn into the war on Germany's side because of the desires of the German invaders and their own fascist governments.

The workers in these countries, led by the communist and workers' parties and despite the cruel terror, began to struggle against the invaders and their puppets during the very first months of the war. The anti-fascist movements in the German occupied countries expanded constantly and took on organization and decisive form in direct relation to the continuing defeats suffered by Germany on the Soviet-German front. Resistance forces switched from acts of sabotage, diversion, and scattered partisan

Sergei Georgiyevich Gorshkov, "Soviet Seamen in the Battles to Liberate the Danube States," *Morskoy Sbornik*, no. 8 (August 1964), pp. 3–13.

excursions to organization of the struggle on a national scale and to the preparation of armed uprisings. The peoples of Rumania, Bulgaria, Yugoslavia, and other countries of southeastern Europe impatiently awaited the Soviet Forces which brought them liberation from the fascist yoke.

* * *

On 20 August 1944, troops of the 2nd Ukrainian Front (General of the Army R. Y. Malinovskiy, commanding) and the 3rd Ukrainian Front (General of the Army F. I. Tolbukhin, commanding) in coordination with the Black Sea Fleet (Admiral F. S. Oktyabrskiy, commanding) switched to an all-out offensive. The Yassy-Kishinev operation—one of the largest strategic operations in the Great Patriotic War—was begun. Our troops, during this operation and in the subsequent development of the offensive, shattered the main forces of the German "Southern Ukraine" Army Group, liberated Soviet Moldavia, and aided the Rumanian and Bulgarian peoples in ridding themselves of the Hitlerite invaders.

The Black Sea Fleet, according to the overall concept for the Yassy-Kishinev operations and the further troop offensive deep into Rumania and Bulgaria, was to employ massed strikes of ships and aviation to paralyze the enemy's fleet at its bases and to interdict his coastal lines of communications. It was to employ naval gunfire and naval and air landings in cooperation with the ground forces in the envelopment and destruction of the enemy's maritime grouping and in the capture of Rumanian and Bulgarian Black Sea ports.

The Danube Flotilla, which was assigned to my command, was given the missions of assisting the 46th Army of the 3rd Ukrainian Front in forcing the Dnestr Estuary, breaking through to the Danube, seizing ports and crossings at the river's mouth and thus block the enemy's maritime grouping from a retreat across the Danube into the depths of Rumania. Further, the flotilla was to provide ferry and river transport for troops and military cargo, clear the river of mines, debark tactical landing forces, and provide gunfire support to troops of the 3rd Ukrainian Front.

The situation at sea at the onset of the operation was wholly favorable for the enemy. The German Rumanian Fleet was significantly inferior to our Black Sea Fleet. After the Hitlerites lost the Crimea and the northwestern shore of the Black Sea, their fleet had port bases only in Rumania and Bulgaria. Nevertheless, the enemy fleet could provide serious opposition to the progress of the operation. It was composed of 1 auxiliary cruiser, 7 fleet destroyers and destroyers, 14 submarines, 23 torpedo cutters, 7 monitors, 3 gunboats, 3 escort ships, 4 mine layers, 25 mine sweepers, and a large number of armed auxiliary ships. A large concentration of enemy aviation was based at fields near Constanza and Satu-Mare.

Significant forces were allocated to execute the tasks assigned the Black Sea Fleet and the Danube Flotilla. These forces included 8 submarines, 41 torpedo cutters, 39 armored cutters, 6 river mine sweepers, 13 patrol cutters, 23 sea sleds, naval infantry units, and coastal artillery. Fleet air forces allocated to the operations were 317 aircraft, including 108 bombers and torpedo bombers, and 29 attack aircraft.

The fleet and flotilla commands paid particular attention to preparing the forces and materiel for the operation. A very great amount of effort was concentrated on the Danube Flotilla which, just prior to that time, had been transferred to the northwestern region of the Black Sea from Azov Sea ports. As a result, the large units, as well as units of the flotilla, were fully prepared to execute the assigned missions.

Inasmuch as combat operations were to be conducted on the territories of other states, the political elements and party organizations in the fleet and flotilla carried on a vast indoctrination program among the seamen so that every seaman would hold high the honor and integrity of the Soviet fighting man.

Combat action in the operations of the Black Sea Fleet began with bombing and strafing attacks against enemy ships in Constanza and Sulina.

A massive air strike by our main forces against Constanza followed on 20 August. Bombers of the 13th Air Division, commanded by Colonel N. Y. Korzunov, were covered by fighters as they sank more than 40 enemy ships and boats. Developing their success, the fleet air force continued to execute strikes against Constanza and Sulina in the following days to 25 August. The mission was a complete success. The enemy fleet was severely weakened (in all 85 ships and boats were sunk or damaged) and it could not offer serious opposition to our offensive during the Kishinev Operation.

Our submarines and torpedo cutters operated against the enemy's lines of communication along the Black Sea's western shores at the same time as aviation was striking at his bases. The submariners and cutter men demonstrated great combat skill and a desire to do everything possible to bring about the earliest defeat of the enemy in the extremely complex situation, made particularly dangerous by the presence of mines.

At the close of 21 August the successful offensive by the main forces of the 2nd and 3rd Ukrainian Fronts necessitated the forcing of the Dnestr Estuary and the encirclement and destruction of the enemy's maritime grouping. This mission was assigned to a group of forces from the 46th Army, the 3rd Ukrainian Front and the Danube Flotilla. Black Sea Fleet aviation was also drawn into the operation.

The group of forces which comprised the landing force included the 83rd and 255th Naval Infantry Brigades, the 3rd Motorcycle Regiment, units of the Novorossiysk Fortified Region, and an amphibious battalion. Overall strength was 8100 men, 10 tanks, 9122 artillery pieces, and 73 mortars. Ships and small craft of the Kerch Armored Cutter Brigade (Brigade Commander, Captain 3rd Rank P. I. Derzhavin) and the 4th River Ship Brigade (Commander, Captain 2nd Rank P. P. Davydov), the 369th Naval Infantry Battalion (Commander, Major S. G. Grigoriev), and a coastal defense sector (Commander, Lieutenant Colonel I. B. Yablonskiy) were allocated from the flotilla's complement for participation in the operation. One dive-bomber and two fighter air regiments were assigned from fleet aviation.

The commander of the group of forces, 46th Army, Lieutenant General A. N. Bakhtin was in command of the operation. I was appointed his Deputy for the naval units.

In consonance with the operational situation and the concept of the operation for debarking the landing force in two areas—Shabo Tyrg and Molaga (northwest and south of the city of Akkerman)—two groups of landing equipment, a cutter detachment for breakthrough to the estuary from the sea, a ship support detachment, a coastal artillery group, and an air group were organized. Cutters of the Danube Flotilla and army sapper boats and ferries were employed as landing craft.

Execution of the operation required tremendous efforts on the part of the forces allocated. Forcing an estuary 10 to 15 kilometers broad and debarking a landing force from a large number of small boats which were not equipped with navigation instruments presented great difficulties. In addition these tasks had to be carried out against the strong opposition of the enemy who had three infantry divisions, a cavalry brigade, and independent units with a significant amount of artillery (27 batteries of 75 to 152-mm caliber and anti-aircraft artillery) on the western shore and in the close-up rear. His forces operated from a system of strong defensive fortifications (concrete and earthen bunkers, barbed wire obstacles, mine fields, etc.). The city of Akkerman (presently Belgorod Dnestrovskiy) was the main defensive strongpoint.

Detailed and purposeful preparation ensured the success of the operation. The landing force units were especially trained in wide water barriers and seizing bridgeheads on the estuaries in the Odessa area. Coastal artillery of the support group registered their fire on the landing sites. The fully ready ships of the flotilla were concentrated in Odessa and landing equipment was transferred to the eastern shore of the Dnestr Estuary under the cover of night.

Political elements and party organizations did much to provide political support for the operation. At party and Konsomol meetings Danube seamen vowed to execute their future tasks with honor.

"We assure our Communist Party," began the resolution of the meeting of the landing force's southern groups, "that we will not quake during the battles and we will carry out the command's order at any price. Communists in the sloops with the landing force will be the first to debark when the enemy shore is reached and by overcoming any opposition by the enemy holding the bank, will resolutely conduct an offensive. Neither danger nor death must halt the execution of the assigned missions."

As darkness fell over the eastern shore of the estuary on 21 August, landing force troops were embarked and combat equipment was loaded onto the landing facilities. At 2340 hours, on signal from my command post at Ovidiopol, the first landing group began its movement toward the western shore of the estuary; the second group followed in its wake. The ships moved in series by march orders, taking their bearings from beacon fires on the estuary's eastern shore.

While the landing groups were under way toward the debarkation points, a detachment of ship-borne artillery support under the command of Captain Lieutenant S. I. Borbot'ko occupied departure positions at the Tsar'gradskiy outlet into the estuary. Ships of the breakthrough detachment, commanded by Hero of the Soviet Union, Captain Lieutenant V. I. Velikiy, also moved to that spot. Armored cutters in the artillery support detachment, and the coastal batteries, opened fire on Bugaz Spit, and our aircraft bombed sectors of the estuary's western shore and the city of Akkerman.

The enemy did not discover our landing groups until they were within 100 to 200 meters of the hostile bank. Heavy fire from artillery pieces, mortars, and machine guns opened immediately on the lead elements of the landing force. The enemy put up the stiffest opposition in the Shabo Tyrg area. Detachments under Senior Lieutenants Yu. M. Korolev and G. H. Kuchevnikov were the first to arrive, and an assault company from the 369th Independent Naval Infantry made an orderly landing. Immediately following this company, the commander of the second landing group, Captain Lieutenant L. P. Potapov, and his chief of staff Captain Lieutenant V. A. Borikov, landed and led the struggle to seize a bridgehead and there to prepare to receive the first and second echelons of the landing force. The seamen of the first landing group, under the command of Captain 3rd Rank A. N. Shal'nov, operated just as skillfully.

With artillery and aviation providing support, units of the lead detachment of the landing force began to move into the depths of the enemy's defense and to expand the bridgeheads seized to the north and south of Akkerman.

The bold and resolute operations of the detachment under Captain Lieutenant V. I. Velikiy greatly facilitated the successful landing. Breaking through into the estuary when the lead landing units were battling for a landing, the ships of the detachment supported them with artillery fire, firing on the enemy gun positions and emplacements in the Akkerman area, and covering the transportation of the 46th Army's landing groups across the estuary.

During the day on 22 August, the main landing forces were moved to the western shore of the Dnestr Estuary where they quickly took up the offensive. Striking boldly, they broke through the enemy's defense over its entire depth, and by evening of that same day they captured Akkerman by storm.

Seamen of the Danube Flotilla demonstrated a high state of combat training, to say nothing of courage and valor in forcing the estuary. They carried out all assigned missions without regard for their lives. The estuary crossing was an example of the smooth cooperation which existed between the Danube Flotilla and the troops of the 3rd Ukrainian Front.

As a result of the successful crossing of the Dnester Estuary, and of landing force operations on the bank, the maritime defense flank was disorganized, the important center of enemy resistance in Akkerman was eliminated, and the requisite conditions for the envelopment and liquidation of his maritime grouping were established.

The enemy did not give up the hope of breaking out of the envelopment and withdrawing along the coastal spit to the Zhebriyany strongpoint and further to the crossings at the mouth of the Danube. In order to prevent this action, a detachment of the flotilla's ships, under command of Hero of the Soviet Union Captain 3rd Rank P. L. Derzhavin, landed a battalion of naval infantry at Zhebriyany on the night of 24 August. Supported by armored cutter fire, and then by assault aviation, the marines, under command of Major F. Ye. Kotanov, captured Zhebriyany.

At dawn the same day, a detachment of ships, commanded by Captain 2nd Rank P. P. Davydov, crossed the Kiliyskiy mouth of the Danube and broke through to the port of Vilkovo. Here, a landing force made up of personnel from the cutters landed and, in coordination with the marines under Major Kotanov, who were advancing from Zhebriyany, captured the port of Vilkovo during the day on 24 August.

Continuing to press the advance, the armored cutters moved up to the Danube and struck at the crossings at Kiliya Staraya and Kiliya Novay. These operations deprived the enemy's groupings along the coast of the capacity to withdraw across the Danube, and they were forced to capitulate.

On 24 August 1944, the troops of the 2nd and 3rd Ukrainian Fronts completed the envelopment of the enemy group at Yassy and Kishinev, a group made up of more than 18 divisions.

Envelopment of the main forces of the German Group of Armies "Southern Ukraine" and the pressing advance of the Soviet Forces deep into Rumania created conditions under which the democratic forces in the country, under leadership of the Communist Party, were able to liquidate the fascist dictatorship of Antonescu, which was hated by the people, and to pull Rumania out of the war and away from Hitlerite Germany.

By 27 August, the Danube Flotilla, in cooperation with troops of the 3rd Ukrainian Front, had successively captured the ports of Kiliya Novaya, Kiliya Staraya, Tul'cha, Reni, Sulina, Izmail, and Galats. Rumanian garrisons, and ships of the river division, resisted only in a few of these ports. For example, in Sulina, after the fascist command's underlings had fled, the base garrison, led by its acting chief Major Kancid Titieni, laid down their weapons in organized fashion and gave up without a battle. By the second day, units of the Slilina garrison were directed into the Tul'cha area for operations against the German forces.

The Rumanian army and navy, despite fanatic resistance from fascist elements in the high command, ever more resolutely turned their weapons against the common enemy—the Hitlerite invaders.

Simultaneously with the occupation of ports on the lower Danube, ships and small craft of our flotilla began to execute the other important mission, that of ferrying troops and combat equipment across the Danube. From 25 August to 5 September 173,957 soldiers and officers of the 37th and 57th Armies, 3rd Ukrainian Front; 340 tanks, 422 tractors, 2204 artillery pieces, 3159 vehicles, and a large quantity of ammunition fuel and foodstuffs were ferried across at Tul'cha and Isakchi.

As soon as the ports at the mouth of the Danube had been liberated, elements of the Black Sea Fleet concentrated in Sulina to capture the Rumanian Navy's main base at Constanza. Troops of the 3rd Ukrainian Front approached Constanza at the same time. The Soviet Naval Command sent an ultimatum to the commander of the Rumanian Navy with a demand that the base and navy be surrendered within one day. The former chief of the Sulina Garrison, Major Kandid Titieni was called on to deliver the ultimatum. This courageous officer was not afraid to appear in Constanza with the order for the Soviet command.

After considering the situation, as well as the desire of the overwhelming majority of the personnel to cease any hostile actions against the Soviet forces, the commander of the Rumanian Navy accepted all the demands imposed by the Soviet Naval Command. Major Titieni, and a pilot, on a torpedo cutter flying a white flag, met our ships as they approached Constanza. Major Titieni actively cooperated in establishing and developing friendly relations between the Rumanian and Soviet soldiers. In 1963, he visited the Soviet Union and was warmly welcomed by the Soviet Veterans Committee.

By the evening of 29 August, a landing force was dropped on a lake near Constanza by Black Sea Fleet aviation and at dawn the next day, torpedo and patrol cutters landed two battalions of naval infantry at the port. The main base of the Rumanian Navy, with all ships, combat equipment, and facilities in it, came under control of Soviet military authorities.

Soviet seamen did everything they could to help the local populace on liberated Rumanian soil to resume a peaceful life and at the same time respected the people's nationalistic feelings and customs.

On 2 September, Soviet forces in pursuit of the retreating German units came to the Rumanian-Bulgarian border. The pro-fascist, Czarist government of Bulgaria continued to cooperate in every way possible with the Hitlerite invaders, thus violating the neutrality they themselves had declared for Bulgaria in the war between Germany and the Soviet Union. Therefore, on 5 September the Soviet Government declared that a state of war existed with Bulgaria.

On 8 September, troops of the 3rd Ukrainian Front crossed the Rumanian-Bulgarian border in the sector from Silistriya to the Black Sea. The Bulgarian people warmly welcomed the Soviet soldier-liberators. Our forces advanced 45 to 50 kilometers the first day, without meeting any resistance from the Bulgarian Army. The ports on the Danube—Silistriya (Silistra), Rushchuk (Ruse), Tutrukay (Tutrukan)—were occupied with the cooperation of the Danube Flotilla.

The arrival of Soviet forces in Bulgaria hastened the uprising of the masses against the fascist-monarchist dictatorship. On 9 September, the Bulgarian people, led by the Communist Party, overthrew the fascist government, and taking authority into their own hands formed the Patriotic Front democratic government.

On that same day, naval and air landing forces, landed by ships and aviation of the Black Sea Fleet occupied the ports of Varna and Burgas. The Hitlerites failed in their barbaric plan to destroy those ports.

On 9 September, the Soviet Government issued an order to all forces to cease military operations against Bulgaria. Bulgaria joined the active struggle against fascist Germany.

Its army took an active role in both the ultimate expulsion of the German invaders from its native land and in the defeat of the Germans in Yugoslavia and Hungary.

The centuries-old friendship of the Russian and Bulgarian peoples entered a new phase of expansion. At a meeting in Sofia, during the visit of a Soviet party and governmental delegation to Bulgaria in May 1962, N. S. Khrushchev said, ". . . the true flowering of our friendship was achieved after 9 September 1944, when Bulgarian workers started on the path of socialist development. Soviet-Bulgarian friendship became truly nationwide and now there are no forces which can suppress it."

Defeat of the German fascist forces in the Yassy-Kishinev operation and the liberation of Rumania and Bulgaria by Soviet troops, decisively altered the military, political and strategic situations on the entire southern wing of the Soviet-German front. Favorable conditions were established for removing Germany's last European ally, Hungary, from the war and for rendering aid to Czechoslovakia and Yugoslavia in the struggle against the fascist invaders. The expulsion of German forces from Rumania and Bulgaria, and the entrance of the latter into the anti-Hitlerite coalition, deprived Germany of important sources of strategic raw materials and foodstuffs, and destroyed her economic ties with Turkey.

The Black Sea Fleet and the Danube Flotilla made a large contribution to the achievement of this noteworthy victory.

As was pointed out above, the various fleet and flotilla forces cooperated with the ground forces in executing the operational missions assigned during the course of combat operations.

Some idea of the results of the fleet and flotilla's combat actions in liberating Rumania and Bulgaria can be gleaned from the following statistics: approximately 50 enemy ships and boats were sunk, and about 150 were captured; the Danube Flotilla ferried and transported more than 290,000 ground force personnel together with weapons, ammunition, rations, and other types of material and technical supplies. The Danube seamen killed more than 2,700 enemy soldiers and officers and took 14,200 prisoners during the operation.

The Supreme High Command gave a high rating to the combat operations of the ships, units, and forces of the Black Sea Fleet and to the Danube Flotilla in the Yassy-Kishinev operation and the liberation of Rumania and Bulgaria. Units and forces which had participated in capturing port cities were awarded the honored titles of Sulina, Tul'cha, Konstanza, Varna, and Burgas. The most outstanding forces and units were awarded the Order of the Red Banner. Hundreds of Black Sea Fleet and Danube Flotilla seamen were honored with high governmental awards—orders and medals of the Soviet Union.

Combat operations in the Black Sea Theatre were concluded with the defeat of the fascist German forces in Rumania and Bulgaria. However, the scope of the armed conflict on the Danube did not diminish. Ahead of the Danube Flotilla lay the drawn out battle to the Austrian port of Linz.

On 28 September, the 3rd Ukrainian Front, in coordination with the Danube Flotilla, troops of Yugoslavia's National Liberation Army, and the Bulgarian Patriotic Front's armies, began an offensive.

The Danube Flotilla ferried and transported troops along the Danube during the preparation period and during the operation. In September–October 1944, units of the 1st Guards Fortified Area, one mechanized corps, three rifle corps, and two rifle divisions with an overall total of 73,000 men together with weapons and combat equipment, were ferried to the Danube ports at Lom, Kalafat, Vidin, and Turnu-Severin; 55,605 men were transported across the Danube.

River men from Rumania, Bulgaria, and Yugoslavia participated in transporting the forces. Rumanian, Bulgarian, and Yugoslavian pilots, who knew the Danube's channels well, took an especially important part in providing transportation.

The flotilla used ship-borne and coastal artillery to provide our advancing forces and units of the 1st Bulgarian Army and the Yugoslavian National Liberation Army with gunfire support, and made tactical landings at Raduevatse, Prakhovo, and Smederovo. The landing at the port of Prakhovo, which was made in daylight, in full view of the stunned enemy, was a particularly bold operation.

Detachments from flotilla cutters, commanded by Heroes of the Soviet Union, Senior Lieutenant M. A. Sokolov and Guards Captain Lieutenant S. I. Borbot'ko, crossed mined obstacles, and the ruined structure of the Belgrade and took a direct part in the battles for the liberation of the Yugoslavian capital and in the capture of a very important German center of resistance in the area between the Danube and Sava Rivers—the city of Zemun. Soviet armored cutters carried the Commander-in-Chief of the Yugoslavian National Liberation Army, Marshal Iosip Broz Tito, and his staff, from the port of Panchevo to Belgrade.

As a result of resolute and skillful operations, Soviet, Yugoslavian, and Bulgarian forces defeated the Hitlerites' Belgrade grouping, and on 20 October liberated Belgrade, the capital of Yugoslavia. Zemun was captured two days later.

Flotilla combat operations in the Belgrade operation were exceptionally difficult. The Danube had been heavily mined by the enemy as well as by British/American aviation. Over 2,700 mines were planted in the middle and lower reaches of the river during the summer and autumn of 1944 alone. In addition, the enemy planted more than 200 mines in the sector from Vidina to Belgrade during the Belgrade operation. Mined obstacles and the many ships sunk by the Germans on the most difficult sectors of the river turned the Danube into a "death road." Navigation on the Danube was complicated further by the fact that the hydrographic and navigational aids were destroyed.

It is for these reasons that the selfless activity of the flotilla's mine sweepers, as well as that of Rumanian and Bulgarian mine sweepers,[1] is particularly noteworthy. The trawlers swept more than 10,000 kilometers in October alone. The coordinated efforts of Soviet, Rumanian, and Bulgarian seamen made the Danube "a road of life."

The Danube Flotilla provided transportation for rations, fuel, construction materials, and other cargoes for Belgrade and the Yugoslavian National Liberation Army in addition to the military transport for the needs of the Soviet forces. Almost three million poods of grain alone were delivered along the Danube, indicative of the selfless aid given Yugoslavia by the Soviet Union.

The government of National Yugoslavia awarded combat medals to a number of seamen in the minesweeper division and its commander, Captain 2nd Rank G. N. Okhrimenko, was honored with the high title of National Hero of Yugoslavia as a token of appreciation for ensuring the safety of vital cargo shipments for the country.

The combat comradeship of the Soviet soldiers, including the Danube seamen, with the soldiers of the Rumanian, Bulgarian, and Yugoslavian armies and river flotillas developed to an even greater extent in the Belgrade operation. Soldiers of the four fraternal countries fought shoulder to shoulder against the hated Hitlerite invaders and did not spare their blood or life itself.

Seamen of the Danube Flotilla demonstrated high standards of military skill, courage and valor in the battles for the liberation of Yugoslavia. By order of the Supreme High Command, the 1st Guards Armored

---

1. Rumanian mine sweepers *Gerdap*, *Bessarab*, *Amurchul*, *Motru*, and *Maykap* and the Bulgarian sweepers *Khristo Botev*, *Vasil' Levskiy*, *Kirill Popov*, and the *Iskar'* participated in sweeping operations in September and October 1944.

Cutter Division was awarded the esteemed title of Belgrade. A large group of seamen were honored with governmental awards.

Defeat of the German fascist forces in Eastern Yugoslavia very much speeded up and facilitated the victory over the enemy in Hungary and Austria.

The flotilla operated with equal intensity in the Budapest (from 29 October 1944 to 13 February 1945) and Vienna (from March to 15 April) offensive operations. Missions executed by the flotilla in the main remained the same: making landings, fire support for ground forces, security for ferries across the Danube, and extended transportation of troops and military cargoes, mine sweeping, etc.

During the advance along the Budapest axis, the flotilla participated primarily in the defeat of the Vukovar enemy grouping based on a system of powerful defensive positions covering the southern approach to Budapest. The flotilla's ships cooperated with the advancing Soviet and Yugoslavian forces with fire from their guns and with landing forces in the Ilok, Opatovets, and Bukovar areas.

Later on the Danube Flotilla participated in the envelopment and defeat of the 188,000 man enemy grouping at Budapest, in repelling Hitlerite attempts to break the blockade of that grouping, and in the liberation of Budapest, Bratislava, and Vienna.

The summary of the results of combat operations of the Danube Military Flotilla in the offensive operations of 1944–45 should note that the flotilla made a substantial contribution to the final victory over the enemy with relatively small forces and facilities. It traveled a route from the Dnestr Estuary and the Danube River mouth to Linz, a distance of over 2,000 kilometers, through battles and with Red Army soldiers. Cooperating with troops of the 2nd and 3rd Ukrainian Fronts and with troops of the Bulgarian and Yugoslavian Armies, the flotilla gave them regular fire support, made 18 landings on the enemy's river flanks, and provided transportation across the Dnestr Estuary, the Danube, and its tributaries for more than 870,000 soldiers and officers, thousands of tanks and self-propelled weapons, tens of thousands of weapons and mortars, hundreds of thousands of vehicles, and a tremendous quantity of rations and other cargoes. The small mine sweeping force in the flotilla, in coordination with the Rumanian and Bulgarian mine sweepers, provided the anti-mine defense for the Danube with their selfless labor.

The flotilla's combat operations were rated highly by the command of the 3rd Ukrainian Front. The Military Council of the Front, in a telegram of greeting on the first anniversary of the flotilla's founding, noted, "The Danube Flotilla fought hand in hand with the 3rd Ukrainian Front's forces from the Dnester Estuary to the capital of Austria, Vienna, and all its missions were successfully carried out, no matter how fraught with difficulties. More than once it broke through enemy fortifications, carried out strikes on the enemy from the rear, and aided the successful assault of the Front's troops."

The Danube Flotilla did so because of the diversified combat experience of its personnel, experience acquired in the preceding war years, because of the mass heroism of its seamen, heroism which was a testimony to their utter dedication to the Communist Party and the socialist Fatherland, because of purposeful party and political work, and because of flexible and efficient control of its forces which was largely due to the flotilla staff, headed by Captain 1st Rank A. V. Sverdlov.

The Soviet government awarded the Danube Flotilla three orders, the Red Banner, Nakhimov, 1st Degree, and Kutuzov, 2nd Degree, for the skillful and resolute actions, courage and heroism of its personnel. Over 7,000 governmental awards were made to Danube seamen for excellence in battles for the liberation of Soviet Moldavia and the Danube countries. Major D. A. Martynov, Senior Lieutenant Ye. G. Larikov, Lieutenants M. A. Sysoyev and N. G. Mochalin, Petty Officer G. M. Agafonov, and Red Navy Man B. B. Muradov were honored with the high title of Hero of the Soviet Union for their especially outstanding feats.

The Danube Flotilla command, in name of the Presidium of the Supreme Soviet of the USSR, awarded orders and medals of the Soviet Union to a large group of Bulgarian, Rumanian, and Yugoslavian soldiers for their resoluteness and courage in the combined battle against the German fascist invaders. Among those decorated were Captain Lieutenant V. I. Pospaleyev, Lieutenant L. B. Gavygov, Warrant Officer N. P. Ovchasov (Bulgaria), Captains 3rd Rank K. Uchanu and K. Krdchunyanu, Senior Lieutenant (now Vice Admiral) S. George (Rumania); Major General M. S. Manola, Colonel M. Yu. Bonachi, Major G. I. Gizdich, Captain M. M. Perishich (Yugoslavia).

The governments of Rumania, Bulgaria, Hungary, and Czechoslovakia awarded orders and medals to a great many Soviet soldiers as an expression of the gratitude of the workers of those countries to their liberators.

Perhaps the most noteworthy result of the participation of Soviet seamen in the 1944–45 operations to liberate the Danube countries was the birth, and strengthening, of their combat comradeship with the seamen of those countries. The seamen from the Black Sea Fleet and the Danube Flotilla were not alone in acquiring combat friends in the persons of Rumanian, Bulgarian, Yugoslavian, and Hungarian seamen. The same type of combat union also arose between the seamen of the Baltic Fleet and the Dnepr Flotilla and the seamen of the Polish National Republic and later with the seamen of the German Democratic Republic.

In the post-war period cooperation between Soviet seamen and seamen of other socialist countries has been further strengthened and has become one of the powerful developmental factors in the navies of those countries.

Soviet seamen, while perfecting their combat mastery and increasing their own navy's combat readiness, have not forgotten to give all the assistance possible to their comrades in arms—the man-of-war's men of Rumania, Bulgaria, Poland and the German Democratic Republic. They share with them the experiences of combat and political training and methods of instructing personnel; they exchange self-entertainment groups and organize sports contests, etc. In recent years our naval vessels have made friendly calls in all the socialist countries, as well as in many other countries. Some of the fraternal countries have been visited several times. Soviet ships have made cruises to Denmark and Yugoslavia this year. Ships of foreign navies have come to the Soviet Union to return calls.

Visits by naval vessels strengthen the mutual trust and fraternity in arms between seamen of the socialist countries and facilitate the expansion of ties and mutual understanding between the peoples of the USSR and the other peace-loving states.

The Soviet people, who are occupied in building communism, value peace and support it, responsibly and firmly. They have felt what war is and well know what suffering it brings to man. The workers of our country unanimously support the Leninist peace-loving policy of the Communist Party and the Soviet Government. However, the imperialists are striving to delay at any cost our progress toward communism.

It is time they understood that the "men of the Soviet Army and Navy, instilled with the spirit of Marxism and Leninism, Soviet patriotism, and socialist internationalism, are at one with the Communist Party and its Leninist Central Committee and are always ready in a single formation with the fraternal socialist countries' armies to shatter any aggressor if that aggressor should dare to attack our Fatherland and the socialist countries."[2]

2. A speech by the USSR Minister of Defense Marshal R. Ya. Malinovskiy at the military parade in Red Square, Moscow, 1 May 1964. *Pravda*, 2 May 1964.

CHAPTER TWO

———————————

Ethos

R ather than recount a single article, this chapter presents a trio of Gorshkov's writings from the 1960s, '70s,
and '80s. The earliest and latest comprise the commander in chief's reports to his navy following the Congress of
the Soviet Communist Party; the second, arguably the most
intriguing insight into his thoughts and frustrations, is a piece
hidden behind a lackluster title about shipboard regulations.

The Party Congress, the KPSS, was the supreme policy-
making body in the USSR, which, after Stalin's death in 1953,
took place once every five years. The 1966 Congress was the
first under Leonid Brezhnev's premiership and, as can be
gleaned from Gorshkov's *Morskoy Sbornik* article, was characterized by outward optimism and bravado. Indeed, Gorshkov toes
the party line for some pages, wallowing in communist rhetoric
of five- and seven-year economic plans, short working days,
and the exploration of space before getting to his central theme
of national security. But that is the point. What Gorshkov does
through his prose is provide a direct link from the international
context and highest level of political decision making to the
day-to-day work of the navy and its people.

Though not directly comparable to Western-style periodic
defense reviews, the same implications can be taken from the
deliberations of the Communist Party Congress. To Gorshkov
the outcomes of the every-five-year gatherings constituted both
an assessment of the global situation and, importantly, orders
to the armed services; he took those assessments and orders and

translated them into objectives for his fleets. Soldiers, sailors, and airmen will fight and die for their friends and comrades, but they will also fight for a cause. Gorshkov helped his men to feel a part of that cause, in this case the national strategy of the Soviet Union and the advance of international socialism, often described in very simple jingoistic terms. In doing so he instilled an ethos.

In his 1966 Congress article Gorshkov praised the Soviet "peace-loving" policies in contrast to the interventionism he saw being pursued by the United States and her allies; he was particularly critical of the use of chemical weapons in Vietnam. He mused on revolutionary technology, perhaps painting a picture of a Russian offset strategy involving missiles, nuclear weapons, and communications, which could defeat Western "aggressors."

Gorshkov made the point that the main mission of the navy was to follow the wishes of the Party—the civilian-military relationship was unambiguous to him, especially the military's subordinate role—and he put the onus on ship and unit commanders to deliver. He implored his sailors to live the ethos of the Soviet state, today largely discredited but then very much alive and well. Parallels can conceivably be drawn to twenty-first-century state and non-state groups that imbue a particular worldview and absolute dedication in their followers. Twenty years after the collapse of the USSR Professor Colin Gray wrote that military forces are often so pre-occupied with the complex and demanding task of organizing themselves that they forget what they are for.[1] In 1966 Gorshkov did not forget, and he did not let his navy forget either.

However, twelve years later in 1978 Gorshkov wrote an altogether more tactical exposition on the underpinning values and principles of Soviet sea power. A five-star invective on the importance of adherence to detailed rules and regulations is, perhaps, not what one might expect from a strategic thinker. Indeed, the second article in this chapter descends at times into rant. That, precisely, is where its significance lies. The Soviet navy of the late 1970s had become stifled by its own bureaucracy and Sergei Gorshkov was sitting atop an organization that was culturally conservative and intellectually constrained. There is no spirit of "mission command" to be found in the words of "Navy Shipboard Regulations—Basis of a Navyman's Service."

It is apparent that Gorshkov recognized that there was a problem but his solution was not to break out of the rut but to reinforce its sides. Dogma had replaced doctrine; the lengthy discussion on the necessity of complying with rules can read like death by a thousand cuts. Nonetheless, there are still traces of good, principled ethos in his writing—his railing against poor leadership made worse by excessive administrative burdens, for example, and his criticism of those who would turn a blind eye, make perfect sense in any age. But the paragraphs that stand out are those that publicly humiliate the officers who fell short of his theoretical ideal. The naming and shaming of the CO who didn't ensure the safety of his ship while at anchor in bad weather, and the CO who allowed rounds' routines to become lax, would not have advanced their careers. However, it may have made others think about their own actions and encouraged them to perform better and avoid a similar fate.

By 1981 Sergei Gorshkov was an old man who had been at the helm of his navy for a quarter of a century. He served a leader, Brezhnev, who was even older and, it turned out, would die the following year. The third article in this chapter, a report following the 26th Party Congress, does not lack propaganda but neither does it contain the same bluster and boasting of the 1960s. The détente of the previous decade was wearing thin, the USSR had invaded and was mired in Afghanistan, and the Solidarity movement in Poland was causing concern about unrest in the country's near abroad. Crucially, the high defense spending of the Cold War was biting. The West had a sound economic base on which to fall back; the East did not. For the Soviet navy there was going to be little extra money.

Gorshkov made clear that the Party Congress was the embodiment of a two-way contract between the state and its various organs. The Party set the direction of travel and the navy would be held to account for its part in delivering the goals. The thrust of his 1981 message was the need for improvement—relative improvement in comparison to NATO navies and absolute improvement against the Soviet fleets' own baseline. As Gorshkov told it, the duty of every serviceman was to strengthen combat readiness, most probably without the luxury of additional resources. The order to "do better" with what you have, to be more "productive," is not uncommon and not always welcome, but it is nearly always warranted.

The final article contains a short critical assessment of NATO exercises and "wasteful" Western defense spending (know thy enemy). In response, Gorshkov argued, the Soviet Union must be alert and he urged an increase in performance brought about by training. He acknowledged that some changes to tactical doctrine were required and encouraged qualitative improvements in individual and collective skills and equipment availability. In particular, he championed the use of focused training teams who could simulate complex conditions, and internal competition to drive standards. If the 1978 article offered a stick to those who fell short, the 1981 article dangled a carrot. He wrote that commanding officers must be taught how to organize competition and that a competitive spirit must be injected into military training in practical ways. It was, he concluded, a "point of honor" that could be reported back to the Party Congress—self-sacrificing, creative effort to strengthen the defensive power of the homeland.

In the twenty-first century we also compete against declining resources and increasing threats, internal change and societal indifference. We see disillusionment, harassment, and, at times, a failure to maintain high professional standards. Building teams of servicemen and women, of officers and enlisted, friends and allies, all held together by a strong, common, underlying ethos, has never been more important. Ethos can be inculcated in many different ways: through education and training, through trust, through words, deeds, and personal example, or through strict adherence to the systematic ways and methods of accomplishing every detail from the most basic task in peacetime to the most complex problem in war. Sergei Gorshkov tried them all and through his writing offers us the opportunity to compare his experiences to our own.

THE XXIIIrd CONGRESS OF THE KPSS AND THE TASKS OF NAVYMEN

Morskoy Sbornik, 1966

The recent XXIIIrd Congress of the Communist Party of the Soviet Union was an important stage in the history of our Party and of the country, in the international Communist movement. It was a tremendous contribution to the work being done in the struggle for Communism.

The Congress served to demonstrate the monolithic solidarity of the KPSS, its unshakable adherence to the mighty banner of Marxism-Leninism, the growing authority of the Party, which is leading the country along the path to progress over the Leninist course. The Communist Party enjoys the unlimited confidence and support of all the people, and full of revolutionary zeal and creative forces, its course is illuminated by the light from Marxist-Leninist theory.

The XXIIIrd Congress reviewed the most important of the questions dealing with the political, economic, ideological, and organizational activities of the Party, and collectively developed its political line for the coming years.

In the summary report of the Central Committee presented to the Congress by L. I. Brezhnev, in the report by A. N. Kosygin concerning the Directives for the new Five-Year Plan for the Development of the National Economy of the USSR, in the remarks made by the delegates, and in the decisions made, is the profound and thorough analysis of the struggle by the Party, by the working class, by the kolkhoz peasant, by the intelligentsia, to bring to life the decisions of the XXIId Congress, of the

Sergei Georgiyevich Gorshkov, "The XXIIIrd Congress of the KPSS and the Tasks of the Navymen," *Morskoy Sbornik*, no. 5 (May 1966), pp. 3–13.

Program of the KPSS; scientific generalizations and conclusions are made and drawn, and the road which the further movement toward Communism is to follow is laid out.

The Congress noted that the years which have passed since the XXIId Congress have been rich in important events. The decisions made by the October (1964), and subsequent, Plenums of the TsK have been of particular significance. They have been of tremendous influence on the entire life of the country, they have lent themselves to the development of scientific principles of Party and State leadership, to an increase in the creative activity of Communists and of all workers, to the affirmation of the Leninist, business-like, realistic approach to the solutions to political and national economic problems. And the Leninist style was characteristic of the Congress itself as well. All of its labors were conducted in an atmosphere of the Bolshevist principled approach, of great demands, of the creative approach to the solution of the problems. The revolutionary spirit, and the political maturity of our Party, appeared with new strength at the Congress.

The Soviet people, led by Lenin's Party, successfully completed fulfillment of the Seven-Year Plan in the period between Congresses. Thanks to new achievements in the national economy, in science, in engineering, and in culture, the Soviet Union has become even mightier in the economic, political, and military sense. Yet another step along the road to the creation of the material and technical base for Communism has been taken. There has been a considerable increase in the volume of industrial production. The technical re-equipping of the most important of the branches of the national economy has been carried out.

An outstanding characteristic of the modern epoch is the unprecedentedly swift development of science. Its influence on all aspects of the material and spiritual lives of society has increased. Our country has a leading place in such of the leading fields of science as nuclear physics, mathematics, metallurgy, electronics, and aircraft building. The entire world has been delighted with the outstanding successes of the Soviet people in studying the universe and in mastering the cosmos. The "Luna-9" automatic station soft landing on the lunar surface was an important step in the investigation of the cosmos, and in the development of interplanetary communications. All the delegates to the Congress heard with delight the playing of the "Internationale" from the universe, transmitted for the first time ever by a moon satellite, the automatic "Luna-10" station.

The specific weight of the Soviet Union's industrial production has increased. The USSR has strengthened its position in the economic competition with the main capitalist countries, and has won new victories. The standard of living of the workers has improved. Important measures have been carried out in regulating and increasing wages in all branches of the national economy. Taxes have been abolished, or reduced, for a great many workers, and pensions for collective farmers have been established. The 7-hour, and in some cases the 6-hour, work day has been introduced. The housing built during the Seven-Year Plan period was almost the equal of that built in all the years of Soviet power up to 1958.

The XXIIIrd Congress laid out before the Party and the people the broad future for the further movement forward along the road of Communist construction. Carrying out the provisions of the new Five-Year Plan will be an important stage in the struggle for the creation of the material and technical base for Communism, and will even further strengthen the economic and defensive might of the country.

An important economic task of the Plan is to ensure the further, considerable, growth of industry and high, stable, tempos of development in agriculture, based on the most complete utilization of the achievements of science and engineering, of the industrial development of the entire social production, of the increase in its effectiveness, of the productivity of labor, and thanks to which there will evolve a substantial rise in the living standards of the people, and a more complete satisfaction of the material and cultural requirements of all of the Soviet peoples.

The KPSS is one of the detachments of international Communism and the workers' movement which has consolidated its position even more. Eighty-eight Communist and workers' parties have united almost 50 million persons in their ranks.

The recent, XXIIIrd Congress was the Congress of the ruling Party of one of the mightiest states in the world, the Soviet Union, which is playing a leading role in the international relations of our day. One of the principle characteristics of the work of the Congress is Leninist internationalism, cordial Bolshevist solidarity with all the countries of socialism, with the Communists of all the world, with all the battlers against imperialism. The KPSS is linked with the other, brotherly Parties by indestructible loyalty to the great teachings of Marx, Engels, and Lenin, to the community of purpose in the struggle for the basic interests of the workers.

Representatives of Communist and workers parties, as well as those from national democratic and left socialist parties from 86 countries throughout the world participated in the work of the Congress. Representatives of 67 parties spoke. Greetings sent to the Congress from yet another 21 countries were published. All of which is indicative of the new, brilliant display of revolutionary, proletarian solidarity, of the fact, that the bonds of brotherhood, of faith and friendship, which join together the Communists and revolutionaries in all countries, are indestructible.

The leaders of delegations from the brotherly parties who spoke at the Congress had great respect for the adherence of the KPSS to the revolutionary Marxist-Leninist theory, to the principle of internationalism, of the tremendous contribution which it has made to strengthening the friendship of socialist nations, of international Communist and workers movements, in the development of the national liberation struggle of peoples. The Congress approved the line, and the practical measures, advanced by the TsK KPSS and which was designed to settle the differences in the international Communist movement on the principle foundation of Marxism-Leninism, the 1957 Declaration, and the 1960 Statement. The Congress also approved the action of the TsK KPSS and the concrete measures undertaken in an effort to settle the differences with the Communist Party of China on the principled foundation of Marxism-Leninism.

The decisions made by the XXIIIrd Congress had for their purpose the further strengthening and development of the world Communist movement. The Congress provided a profound and multi-faceted characterization of the international situation, and noted the intensification of the danger of war, occasioned by the increase in the aggressiveness of American imperialism. The facts prove that the relationship of the forces in the world arena continue to change in favor of socialism, of the worker and national liberation movement. Imperialism, because it does not wish to come to terms with the inexorable course of history, is striving to recover the positions it has lost, to prevent social progress on all continents. The imperialists, and particularly the United States, are falling back more and more openly and brazenly on the weapon of provocation and aggression, striving in this way to find a way out of the difficulties and contradictions with which the world capitalist system is confronted.

In the twenty years since World War II ended the United States has spent 48 times more money on military needs than was the case for the twenty years preceding that war. Today over three-quarters of all expenditures in the United States federal budget go to the military, directly or indirectly. It is the fault of the Pentagon that the dark clouds of the atomic threat grow ever thicker over mankind. The aggressive nature of American imperialism is demonstrated with particular clarity in the criminal war against the Vietnamese people. Peaceful cities and villages in the Democratic Republic of Vietnam have been subjected to barbarous bombardment by the Americans, who use napalm, toxic gases, and other inhuman means of destroying people.

The Congress, in its Statement concerned with United States aggression in Vietnam, proclaimed its brotherly solidarity with the heroic Vietnamese people, with the Workers Party of Vietnam, with the National Liberation Front of South Vietnam. The Congress, in the name of all Communists and of the Soviet people, categorically demanded the cessation of aggression in Vietnam, the withdrawal of all interventionist troops, and appealed to all Communist and workers parties to even more staunchly strive for unity of action in the struggle against American aggression, to provide effective help and support for the Vietnamese people.

The delegates to the Congress, and the representatives of the brotherly Communist and workers parties, laid bare before the entire world the vandalism of the American imperialists in Vietnam, unanimously supported the measures being taken by the TsK KPSS and the Soviet government in providing material, economic, and military assistance to the Vietnamese people in their just struggle.

In Europe, West German imperialism is advancing as the principal ally of the United States. West Germany is more and more becoming the breeding ground for the danger of war, what with the revanchist passions seething in that country.

The TsK KPSS, in establishing its foreign policy line, takes into consideration the entire complex of the international situation. The USSR consistently conducts a policy of peace, a policy the essence of which flows from the very nature of the socialist state and which is determined by the interests of the workers.

In today's complex international conditions, the Party is displaying a tireless concern for the further strengthening of the defensive might of our

Motherland. It considers this to be its most important task. The Congress demanded further improvement in the production of defense equipment in order that the Soviet Army and Navy have the most powerful and modern of armaments.

Thanks to success in the development of the economy, of science and engineering, our Army and Navy have been equipped with the most modern of nuclear weapons and the latest models of military equipment. A far-reaching, scientific, military doctrine for the Soviet state has been developed, the basis for which has been the instructions from the TsK KPSS and the government.

The tempestuous growth in scientific and technical progress has made possible the rebuilding of all branches of the Armed Forces on a new technical base. And the Navy too has had a qualitative renewal of its equipment. Atomic energy, automation, and electronics have been widely developed. The main propulsion installations of the Navy's warships have undergone truly revolutionary changes. There has been a several-fold, recent, increase in the amount of propulsion power available in submarines, and this has resulted in a considerable increase in their submerged speeds. Modern radio and electronics equipment for communications and accurate navigation provide for reliable cruising of combatant ships anywhere on the world ocean, for effective utilization of weapons, for the control of fleet forces and equipment.

The development of nuclear weapons, and of the rockets used to deliver them, has played a basic and revolutionary role, one which has led to a sharp increase in the combat capabilities of the fleet and to a change in the forms and methods of using it in armed combat.

Submarines equipped with atomic propulsion combine in themselves such qualities as secrecy, mobility, virtually unlimited cruising range, and colossal striking power, and rightfully occupy a leading place in the struggle with the surface and submarine forces of the enemy, as well as being able to stand off at vast distances and strike vitally important ground targets on the enemy's territory.

The fleet has been joined by new missile ships with equipment which can search out, track, and destroy modern submarines; they have long-range homing missiles for use against surface combatant ships, as well as controlled anti-aircraft missiles for defense against air enemies. These warships are, in many of their tactical characteristics, on a par with the best achievements of the world's naval shipbuilders. They are capable of carrying out important combat missions in the struggle with the enemy's naval forces.

The Navy has created naval missile-carrying aviation, the primary weapons for which are missiles which can fly long distances. Highly maneuverable naval infantry units, worthy successors to the legendary heroes of the Great Patriotic War, are being developed.

Unified views with respect to the tasks the fleet will have in modern war, as well as with respect to the methods for conducting naval operations, have been developed, and have issued from the general, axiomatic provisions of Soviet military doctrine.

Because of the technical refit given the fleet we have, in recent years, become capable of switching to what is qualitatively a new type of combat training; the performance of daily service in outlying regions of the world ocean. The training is conducted in the form of large-scale exercises, under the complex conditions of being separated from base. The practice of combat training, and of long cruises, is indicative of the excellent quality of Soviet engineering, of the high level of training, and of the moral and combat qualities of personnel. Past, large-scale exercises of fleets in conjunction with Soviet Army troops have shown that the Navy is capable of carrying out the complex missions of modern war.

The basic wealth of our fleet is its command cadres, cadres which are unequivocally committed to the work of the Communist Party and to the socialist Motherland. Over 90% of all the officers serving on board ship have higher educations. All submarine commanders have a higher education, and many of them have academic qualifications. Two-thirds of Force commanders have completed the Academy. The specific weight of the engineering and technical cadres has increased considerably, and today they make up over half of the officer corps. Some 90% of the officers are Communists and Komsomols. Today every fifth fighting man in the Navy is a Communist.

The young replacements reporting to the fleet are better, qualitatively speaking, each year. Today there are twice as many young sailors with a middle education as there were 10 years ago, and 91% of the sailors and petty officers have higher, middle, or incomplete middle educations. 84% of the young sailors report with technical specialties, making it possible to train good military specialists in short order.

In response to the concern of the Party and of the government for the VMF, the awarding to all the Fleets of the Order of the Red Banner, personnel during drills and exercises, on long cruises, augment the glorious military traditions of the older generation, and they carry out their duties with a sense of high responsibility.

Together with all the Soviet people, the Navymen have confronted the Congress of their native Party with worthy deeds. Standing their pre-Congress watches, they obtained good marks in combat and political training, they increased their successes in missile firings. The number of *otlichniks*,[1] rated specialists, and excellent combatant ships and units, has increased. Today over half of the VMF personnel are *otlichniks* and rated specialists. They make up 80 to 90% of the crews of atomic submarines and missile ships. Many Navymen have been honored with governmental awards for a high degree of military skill and exemplary fulfillment of command assignments. Among them are Captain 2d Rank V. A. Gridnev, Engineer-Captain 2d Rank O. D. Bobyrev, Colonel A. P. Shul'zhenko, Major General I. T. Yaramyshev, and others. On some of the submarines all the officers, petty officers, and sailors have been selected for governmental awards. Captain 1st Rank Salop, and Captains 2d Rank Ust'yantsev and Bezhanov, were delegates to the XXIIIrd Congress and serve in a ship, the crew of which received high marks in combat and political training.

An important gift to the Congress was made by the submariners in the group of atomic submarines under command of Rear Admiral A. I. Sorokin, which successfully made an around the world cruise. The submarines covered almost 25,000 miles submerged. The men displayed a high degree of combat training and skill, successfully carried out all training and combat and special missions, and demonstrated high moral and combat qualities, clear-cut organization, and amenability to discipline. Particularly outstanding on the cruise were Detachment Commander A. I. Sorokin, submariners I. Gayvoronskiy, R. Putilov, V. Tereshkov, G. Mironenko, Usenko, and others.

The XXIIIrd Congress of the KPSS gave the Soviet Armed Forces, and this includes the Navy, the extremely important and responsible

---

1. *Otlichnik*—one who has obtained excellent results in combat and political training.

missions of further improving their combat readiness, of increasing their unremitting vigilance, so that they will also be ready to reliably protect the achievements of socialism and inflict a crushing rebuff to any imperialist aggression.

We are faced today by a coalition of imperialist powers, the leading places among which are occupied by the so-called traditional sea powers. In their preparations for a new world war our probable enemies, in devoting a tremendous amount of attention to the development of all branches of the Armed Forces, are assigning a special role to their fleets. Over one-third of all the strategic nuclear weapons available to all branches of the armed forces are concentrated in the American fleet at this time. Today, as never before in history, there is an unprecedented concentration of striking power in the sphere of operation of the fleet, and the role of combat operations at sea in the course of armed struggle is always on the increase. This compels us to continuously increase the combat might and the combat readiness of the Navy.

It is important that our analysis of the activity of the Military Councils, of all commanders and political organs, be profound and adroit, with Party demands taken into consideration, that the leadership of fleet forces, of all links in the complex fleet organism, be raised to the highest possible level.

The officer corps of the fleet must work with initiative, and creatively, with a sense of high responsibility, to obtain effective and quality fulfillment of assigned missions. Reduce the time required to get fleet forces combat ready; add combatant ships accepted from the builders to the fleet within the fixed periods of time; improve operational, tactical, and special training.

We must be firmer in getting rid of the conventional, and of over simplification, in combat training, in disregard for secrecy, in underestimations in the training of troops to act under conditions when the enemy has used mass destruction media.

In order to bring to life the requirements of the XXIIIrd Congress with respect to strengthening defense capabilities, it is necessary that all commanders, political organs and Party organizations, concentrate their attention on living organizational work right on board the ships and in the units.

The recent Congress condemned subjectivism, and demanded that there be an increase in the role of scientific leadership. This is directly applicable to those who lead military cadres as well. V. I. Lenin said that without science it is impossible to build a modern Army and Navy. In the new stage of development of the Soviet Army and Navy life is urgent in demanding of all our officers, admirals, and generals, a profound study of the behavior patterns involved in the development of society, of the laws of armed struggle, of the theory and practice of military affairs, in order for them to be able to use to the fullest the skills which permit them to intelligently teach and indoctrinate their subordinates.

It is important that all officers, admirals, and generals constantly maintain their political and military knowledge at the contemporary level, that they follow developments in military theory and combat techniques, that they display more initiative in developing new procedures and methods for the combat utilization of fleet forces. This is the way in which we must indoctrinate the leaders, particularly those in command of ships, of units, in order that they not be at a loss, regardless of the situation, that they exhibit independence, that they take well-grounded decisions, and are morally ready to bear full responsibility for their actions and for the orders they issue.

The demands of the Party Congress levied on the Soviet scientist are equally pertinent with respect to the workers in the VMF scientific and research institutes. The interests of combat readiness demand an operational solution to urgent problems, an active introduction of the latest achievements of science and engineering into the building of the fleet, an organic connection between theory and experience in combat training.

The role of Party and political work as one of the most important conditions for the successful construction of the Armed Forces, for the strengthening of the organization of the service and of discipline, for increasing the combat might of the Army and the Navy, is increasing. It is useful for all of us to recall the words of M. Z. Frunzye that political work is a new form of weapon, a weapon to be feared by any of our enemies. The political organs in the forces, and the Party organizations on board the ships, and in the units, ought to become the combat organizers and indoctrinators of personnel, putting into practice persistently and in a qualified manner the decisions of the Communist Party, with a thorough grasp of all aspects of combat training and service. Modernization of leadership in the primary Party organizations is to be pressed in order that they strictly observe the Leninist norms of Party life and that they all work actively and purposefully.

Experience in the leading ships and units indicates that the training and indoctrination of personnel is most successful where the commander, who is the man who embodies the single-command concept, the political workers and the Secretary of the Party organization, work in friendship and in a business-like manner. The mature such commander is always interested in seeing to it that the Party organization works energetically, that its authority has constant growth. The political organs in the forces ought to better educate commanders in the ability to be supported in their actions by the Party organization.

The moral factor plays an unusually great part given the conditions which prevail in modern war. Indoctrinating fighting men with Communist ideology and Soviet patriotism, with high political and moral qualities, is the primary task of commanders' political organs and Party organizations in the fleet. The XXIIIrd Congress has demanded that ideological work be a matter for all Communists, for the entire Party.

Of tremendous significance in agitation and propaganda work is the struggle with the bourgeois ideology, the unmasking of the aggressive essence of American imperialism, the indoctrinating of hatred for the enemies of socialism and with a high degree of vigilance. And this can only be done by intensifying the military and patriotic indoctrination of fleet youth. Indoctrination work within the Party proper is taking on tremendous importance. Communists are men of high moral substance, and this is what cements the unity of Communism in ranks, increases combat capabilities, makes the Communist a purposeful, true organizer and a political battler. The Party organizations are obligated, to increase the demands imposed on Communists, to intensify control over their political training, to draw them into active political and indoctrinational work.

The Central Committee's summary report discusses the need for personal, active participation of Communist leaders in ideological work. This is of particular importance now when fighting men, workers, and employees of the fleet are studying the materials and decisions of the XXIIIrd Congress of the KPSS. There is today no more important and responsible task than propaganda dealing with the materials and the decisions of the Congress, and making them a reality, and this is true for Communists and even more so for the leaders.

The Navymen must be helped in finding out what their part is in meeting the demands of the Party Congress. The Party organizations are called upon to do everything in their power to see to it that each sees in the assignments of the Five-Year Program his personal effort, and that he does his proper share in carrying it out.

Our Party is preparing to greet the 50th anniversary of the Great October Socialist Revolution and the 100th anniversary of the birth of V. I. Lenin properly. So now is the time to turn detailed organizational and ideological work in this direction.

The recent Congress of the KPSS has demanded of Party, Soviet, and military cadres, further strengthening of Party and state discipline. "The task," states the summary report of the TsK KPSS, "is to increase the sense of responsibility of every Communist for the state of affairs in his organization, and in the Party as a whole; to be demanding of all members of the Party, and permit no liberalism with respect to those who violate Party and state discipline, who forget their Party obligations, and who feel that belonging to the Party ought to give them some sort of privilege."

These instructions are of particular importance to the Soviet Armed Forces, in which firm military discipline and personal responsibility for assignments is the basis for the constant readiness of the troops to protect the Socialist Motherland. Military discipline is very much dependent on the personal example, and on a high degree of performance by officers, particularly by commanders who embody the single-command concept. Unfortunately, one can still meet officers who display liberalism and weak will with respect to subordinates, and who themselves sometimes permit lack of discipline to appear. The Military Councils, commanders and political organs must intensify their work with the leading officer cadres, striving while so doing to attain a high sense of responsibility, personal example, and ability to perform as characteristic traits of each officer, regardless of the sector in which he may be found. And staffs too must become greatly involved in questions of departmental organization and of strengthening discipline. It is mandatory that staff officers, when working on board ship, and in a unit, take an interest in departmental organization, in discipline, as well as in engineering, tactics and special training, for without the former a constant, high degree of combat readiness is unthinkable.

The principled approach and exactingness on the part of Party and Komsomol organizations are the most important conditions for strengthening discipline. They should be put into practice on board every ship, and in every unit, in complete response to the demands of the Party Congress.

The XXIIIrd Congress has been a signal event in the life of our Party, of the people, of the fighting men in the Armed Forces. The materials and the decisions of the Congress carry a powerful mobilizing charge; they will prove to have a tremendous influence on all aspects of Communist construction and on the strengthening of the defensive capabilities of the Soviet Motherland. Putting into practice the instructions of the Party with respect to increasing vigilance, combat readiness, and strengthening discipline, is the main mission of the Military Councils, commanders, political organs and Party organizations in the Navy.

NAVY SHIPBOARD REGULATIONS— BASIS OF A NAVYMAN'S SERVICE

Morskoy Sbornik, 1978

As a result of the grandiose socio-political and economic achievements of our Motherland, the Navy, together with the other services of the Armed Forces of the USSR, has undergone profound qualitative changes during the last decade. Equipment and weapons have been improved and have become more complex; and as naval operations have developed there have occurred corresponding changes in the content of military regulations, through which the influence of our party, government, and military thought are exerted on the training and indoctrination of personnel and on military life as a whole.

The year 1977 saw the adoption of our new Constitution, the Basic Law of the Union of Soviet Socialist Republics defining the obligations of the Soviet people in connection with the defense of the Fatherland and the

Sergei Georgiyevich Gorshkov, "Navy Shipboard Regulations—Basis of a Navyman's Service," *Morskoy Sbornik*, no. 5 (1978), pp. 3–7.

entire socialist commonwealth against possible encroachments on the part of an aggressor.

All this has required the partial revision and changes in a number of provisions of the Navy Shipboard Regulations of the Navy of the Union of Soviet Socialist Republics. Ships, units, and forces will receive the new regulations in the near future.

The Navy Shipboard Regulations are a collection of immutable laws governing naval service. They represent the active experience of more than one generation of Navymen, experience tried and proven in countless naval cruises and campaigns and in fierce battles and engagements, experience carefully collected, bit by bit, and included in the concise lines of the articles they contain. They are the original source and basis of all manuals, handbooks, and rules developing and defining in their diversity all aspects of the life of naval units, their organization and training, as well as of the daily performance of duty and the shipboard regulations.

At the dawn of the formation of the Russian Navy, the actions of the commanders of Peter's ships were based on regulations. Precise fulfillment of regulation requirements determined to a great extent the victorious outcome of the battles engaged in by the squadrons of Spiridov, Ushakov, Lazarev, and Nakhimov. From the fires of revolution issued a revolutionary naval order. It was tempered in the Civil War, when the glorious sailors of October again proved their worth with those powers of organization which were so highly valued by the great Lenin. The Red Navy Regulations cemented the service and military operations of naval personnel during the terrible years of the Great Patriotic War, throughout which the navy fulfilled its duty to the Motherland.

Together with the navy, the Regulations too have covered a great course, absorbing everything new and vitally necessary and sweeping away that which has become outdated and obsolete. Even now the life and service of personnel aboard ships and vessels flying the flag of the Navy of the Union of Soviet Socialist Republics are based on the Navy Shipboard Regulations, and their requirements are obligatory for everyone who sets foot on their decks.

There is no aspect of the activity of naval personnel which would not be reflected in the Navy Shipboard Regulations. They cover shipboard organization and military training, the routines of service and daily life, the maintenance of ships, ensuring their survivability and maintaining them in repair, and the performance of shipboard duties. They set forth the duties of all service personnel, from the seaman to the ship and force commander. Here one can find the answer to practically any question concerning shipboard regulations.

To live by the regulations means to organize service in such a way that a change in a situation at sea or on a cruise, at anchor or on the mooring lines, that any tactical problem or mission comes as no surprise for a crew. To live by the regulations means to instruct and indoctrinate personnel so that all requirements of complex and varied naval service are fulfilled punctually and precisely; for without this, to accomplish the tasks of military and political training would be impossible. To live by the regulations is constantly to maintain oneself in the highest degree of combat readiness.

The original cause of shortcomings in the performance of individual service personnel is always to be sought in their ignorance of, or failure to abide by, one provision or another of the regulations. Similarly, measures to remedy shortcomings which have been discovered should be prescribed in accordance with their requirements. It should always be remembered that one who thoroughly knows and strictly abides by the Navy Ship-board Regulations, who has indoctrinated and taught his subordinates to observe them, is one who tolerates no violations, since the Regulations exist for the purpose of ensuring successful, and only successful, service. Nonobservance—that is the main cause of the occurrence of individual omissions and deficiencies.

Cases of a person's willful, premeditated violation of the military order are rare in our military environment. Failure to abide by the Regulations is much more often the result of a lack of self-possession, of that strict self-discipline which all military personnel must have. For as a rule, the loss of a sense of responsibility begins with insignificant instances of self-indulgence, after which inevitably follow concessions to others. It is in precisely such an atmosphere of connivance and mutual condonation on the part of military personnel that there occasionally arise doubts concerning one's duty to comply with Regulation requirements along with such notions, impermissible, in military service, as: "Do I really have to do this, when I can get out of it by . . ." Self-centered urges and efforts to avoid "needless" trouble win out over a sense of duty and responsibility. Little by little these service personnel accustom themselves to the idea that there is nothing especially wrong with some deviations from the Regulations, provided that everything turns out all right. And sometimes it does. But such presumptuousness and the irresponsibility to which it leads are more often brought to a turning point by serious, unpleasant developments.

For example, one of the minesweepers of the Black Sea Fleet found itself in a difficult situation during a period of cold weather. This need not have happened had the ship commander, Captain Lieutenant V. Rodin, performed his duty as prescribed by the Regulations and taken timely precautionary measures to ensure the security of the ship's anchorage with the change in the weather and required of the watch greater vigilance and closer observation of the situation in the roads. But he deviated from the requirements of the Naval Regulations and paid dearly for it.

In no case is it possible to divide the provisions of the Regulations into those which are important and must therefore be observed, and those which are unimportant and can, in the opinion of some military personnel, be done without. There is nothing more dangerous than a complacent attitude toward such reasoning. In organizing an effort to achieve adherence to Regulations, it should always be kept in mind that naval service as a whole makes its educational impact only when aboard ships and in subunits these Regulations are adhered to in all things, great and small, and when any violation of Regulation procedures is subjected to thorough and principled analysis.

In his article "Company Doctrine," F. Engels warned that "any deviation from regulation procedure is inevitably connected with certain breaches of discipline and a lack of consistency, which not only make one the beholder an impression of slipshodness, but it also presumes a certain loss of time and forces a soldier to the conclusion that individual sections of the regulations are pure nonsense."[1]

Failure to abide by the regulations is sometimes a result, however paradoxical it may seem, of administrative zealousness. Some chiefs and commanders are carried away by written directives; they love to invest everything they say with the form of a written order. And so an endless stream of paper flows into the subunit. As a result, people simply begin to wave it aside. Such an "administrative paper itch" not only does not

---

1. F. Engels, "Izbrannyye voyennyye proizvedeniya," *Voyenizdat*, 1957, p. 421.

discipline people, but, on the contrary, leads them away from a thorough study and strict observance of the basic laws of military life. They begin to forget about the Regulations and more and more seldom turn to them. However, much of what these written directives contain is already written in the Regulations, and more clearly and concisely at that.

We should not permit unnecessary duplication of provisions of the Regulations, find substitutes for the requirements they impose, or interpret them in an arbitrary manner. For all this leads in the end to disparagement of the role played by the Regulations, to neglect of their provisions, and does not accustom military personnel to turn to them in the first instance.

Respect for the Regulations should be instilled from day to day, patiently and persistently, so that their ideas and requirements become personal convictions of all naval personnel and develop into personal habit with them. But the important thing at this point is personal example, constant supervision, and a high level of exactingness in all aspects of life aboard a ship. Exacting demands discipline people and help them see their shortcomings more clearly and eliminate them in a timely manner.

The Regulations provide exhaustive answers to the questions of what, when, and how to check. But the misfortune of some commanders and chiefs is that they sometimes forget about this. One fails to conduct the prescribed inspections and reviews; another does not find the time to make the rounds of all quarters on the ship and personally satisfy himself that everything is in proper working order; a third fails to check into how an order he has issued has been carried out.

On a ship of the Northern Fleet on which Captain Lieutenant V. Peregudov is serving, deficiencies were recently observed in the maintenance of equipment and certain service and living quarters. It turned out that nobody had even taken a look in there for a long time. And typically it is the case that the petty officers and officers responsible for the condition of these quarters have no poor knowledge of the Regulation requirements governing the procedure and intervals for inspecting their administration; it is only that they have not accustomed themselves and their subordinates to the strict observance of these requirements and have not created on the ship an atmosphere in which a failure to observe them would simply be unthinkable.

To remember the letter of the Regulations and to know all their sections and articles is still only half of the matter. It is important to ensure that each member of the crew consistently put them into practice and that the conduct and duty performance of all personnel are in strict conformity with their requirements. The commander of the ship, of course, must serve as an example of this; for he is the one who has been called to be the leading standard-bearer in the cause of the observance of regulations, of the inviolability of an order based on regulation procedures, and in an uncompromising manner to demand the same from others.

If a commander underestimates the importance of precise, unfailing implementation of the provisions of the regulations, if he permits a free interpretation of them, and sometimes fails to notice one or another breach of discipline or departure from regulation procedures, it means that he is not sufficiently demanding. Soviet military regulations, including the Navy Shipboard Regulations, consider exactingness a vital obligation of every commander. The right to exercise command over people which is granted a commander by the Party and the Government confers not only authority, but great responsibility as well. Appearing in the forefront at this point is the critical attitude on the part of an officer, warrant officer, or petty officer towards himself. Without a deeply conscious sense of the responsibility which rests on them, and without a great degree of self-possession and constant self-control, unit and subunit commanders cannot count on success in leading their subordinates and establishing procedures prescribed by regulations.

As a rule, of course, the absolute majority of our commanders notice all departures from the regulation standards of life and react properly to them. True exactingness on the part of a commander is invariably connected with a display of persistence, patience, volition, organizing ability, and an active relationship to the performance of party and military duties. There are cases, however, in which the same unit has one subunit commander who is demanding in all things, while another is indulgent. Service on one ship is organized in accordance with regulation procedures, while on another there are departures from these procedures. This produces in insufficiently disciplined military personnel an unhealthy state of mind and creates the likelihood of deviations from the Regulations.

A high degree of exactingness in exercising his command over an order based on adherence to Regulation procedures is an indispensable condition for the mutual relationships between commanders and their subordinates. Exacting commanders are usually respected and are viewed as people who know their job, who are firm in their decisions, and on whom it is always possible to rely.

Experience shows that contributing to the direction and maintenance of a firm order aboard a ship, in addition to the great degree of exactingness on the part of personnel in positions of authority, are well organized political and military education and properly disciplined training. Clarification, conviction, and heightened awareness assume a constant appeal to the consciousness, to the sensitivities of people. Naval personnel should understand why it is necessary strictly and unquestioningly to fulfill the requirements of the Regulations. Departures from the Regulations are frequently to be explained, not by deliberate actions on the part of those who are directly at fault, but rather they occur as a result of a lack of understanding or an improper execution on their part of the provisions of naval law.

Upon inquiry, it was found that on the ship on which officer I. Kalugin is serving there were certain personnel who did not know the letter symbols marking doors, hatches, manhole hatches, and the shut-off mechanisms of the ship's ventilation system and specifying their position for conditions of readiness and alerts, and so naturally could not follow the procedures for closing them. As it turned out, they did not even have an idea of what such a situation could lead to. The commanders involved should have explained in a timely manner the purpose for and the sequence involved in closing and sealing the openings in the hull of a ship and the serious consequences which may be produced by departures from these rules.

It is important to remember that the words of a teacher achieve their purpose only if they are not at variance with deeds, if a seaman sees a practical confirmation of what he has been told. It is therefore extremely necessary that explanation be followed by the well-organized fulfillment of requirements. This should make certain that a military man knows how to perform his duty. V. I. Lenin declared that fine words are lost if they are not contained within the iron limits of the deed.

A structure and tenor of military life created in strict conformity with the requirements of the Regulations comprise the main prerequisite for any strengthening of discipline and order aboard a ship or in a unit or subunit. Only when they find themselves in the atmosphere of an exemplary military order are seamen convinced of its purposefulness and firmness.

However, one may explain and attempt to persuade only up to the point at which the question becomes one of carrying out an order. No discussion or disputation are now admissible. As M. V. Frunze declared, "Persuasion and exhortation to carry out orders are, by themselves, a most flagrant breach of discipline."[2]

To master and establish adherence to regulation procedures aboard a ship must be accomplished in a well planned, constant, and purposeful manner and requires as well the accomplishment of military and political training tasks. It should not be a campaign, an accelerated stage in a sequence advancing toward the preparation for and taking of another examination. The Regulations may be mastered and adherence to them established only if they are kept in mind and observance of them is required every day, every hour, at sea and in port, on duty, in training, and during off-duty time.

A great and immediate effect on the organization, manner, and strengthening of discipline is exerted by a strict adherence to the daily routine. Strictly and precisely following the daily routine ensures coordination and organization in the activities of personnel and increases their responsibility and discipline. These are the very qualities necessary for the successful training of naval personnel under any conditions. Experience confirms that even insignificant departures from regulation requirements may seriously disrupt the normal life of the ship or a subunit, affect the training process, and, in the final analysis, have a negative influence on its effectiveness. The daily routine is therefore considered the basis of the life and activity of shipboard personnel and control over its observance is the very first duty of officers and on-duty personnel. The daily routine and the performance of shipboard duties are the fundamental bases of a ship's organization and provide the basic framework of shipboard life as a whole, as well as of the training and life of the crew. Performance of duties aboard ship is a daily teacher and a supervisor and guardian of a regulation-based organization. That is why it is so important in the course of studying and introducing the Regulations to devote the most constant attention to training and the complete fulfillment of their responsibilities by those charged with the performance of shipboard duties.

---

2. M. V. Frunze, "Izbrannyye proizvedeniya," *Voyenizdat*, 1965, p. 221.

Training in preparation to enter upon the performance of duties, testing knowledge of duties, mustering the watch in strict conformity with the regulations, and strict control over the uniform appearance of personnel provide a guarantee of good training and first-rate performance of shipboard duties. This is a daily school for learning the Regulations for all personnel which, with the proper organizations and supervision, provides the maximum in knowledge and skills.

In training personnel for performance of shipboard duties in conformity with the regulations it is necessary systematically to conduct instruction and training in establishing an organization of duties, this to include demonstrational measures. One may be strict in one's requirements but still not obtain the proper performance. One may study the provisions of the Regulations and yet implement them improperly. It is only when such study includes explanation and demonstration, and implementation exactingness and supervision, that it is possible to develop in personnel the requisite ability to perform their duties quickly, efficiently, and in strict conformity with the Regulations.

To organize the life and work of a crew in strict accordance with the requirements of the Regulations and to maintain strict adherence to military procedures are the most important task of a ship's command. Called upon to render great assistance in this regard to commanders at all levels are their staffs, political organs, and party and Komsomol organizations. Their duty is to mobilize all naval personnel for solid mastery of and strict adherence to the provisions of the Regulations and to try to achieve on the part of service personnel a clear understanding of their duty fully and consciously to observe all their requirements.

"Serving as a solid cementing force in military units," declared Marshal of the Soviet Union D. F. Ustinov, Minister of Defense of the USSR, "are the party organizations and their military assistant, the army Komsomol. Communists and Komsomol members are a great force and a reliable point of support for commanders in accomplishing the tasks involved in raising the level of combat readiness of subunits, units, and ships, and improving discipline and organization."[3]

Also necessary for the maintenance of a solid, regulation-based organization are a high level of organizational work on the part of all officers,

---

3. *Krasnaya Zvezda*, 23 February 1978.

their constant exactingness toward subordinates, and an uncompromising attitude toward deficiencies. Experience indicates that success in service accompanies him who conducts his educational and organizational activities in inseparable unity. Success also depends on the ability of commanders and chiefs to utilize the force of public opinion in the effort to improve discipline and to organize constant control over the activities of their subordinates.

Purposeful publicity of Regulation requirements and their thorough mastery will create the requisite preconditions for the successful accomplishment of the tasks involved in military and political training, a steady increase in the mastery of military skills, the improvement of discipline, the organization of personnel, achievement of the goals set for socialist competition, and implementation of the decision of the 25th Congress of the CPSU.

Absolute, efficient and precise fulfillment of the requirements of the Regulations and the organization of the daily life and activities of the Navy in full accordance with their letter and spirit will make it possible to maintain ships, units, and forces in constant combat readiness and guarantee an immediate rebuff to any aggressor.

This is in full accord with one of the most important provisions of the Constitution of the Union of Soviet Socialist Republics dealing with the defense of the socialist Fatherland.

THE 26TH PARTY CONGRESS

Morskoy Sbornik, 1981

The path which has been traveled by the Navy from the 25th Party Congress to the 26th is a path of indefatigable military endeavor on the part of seamen and petty officers, warrant officers, commissioned officers, admirals and generals, who are devoting all their efforts, knowledge and experience to selfless service of their Motherland and to exemplary performance of their military duty.

Sergei Georgiyevich Gorshkov, "The 26th Party Congress," *Morskoy Sbornik*, no. 1 (1981), pp. 3–8.

Together with the Soviet people as a whole, our Navymen, as the 26th CPSU Congress begins, are rallying around the Party of Lenin. They consider it their primary mission, to defend vigilantly all that has been built and accomplished by our people, to strengthen our Armed Forces and to increase in every way possible our Homeland's defense capacity; and they are accepting this mission as a program for action, devoting all their military labors to its execution.

Thanks to the unflagging concern of the Party and the Government in the years since the 25th Congress, our Navy has been supplied with new generations of fighting ships to replace those which have outlived their usefulness. We are proud of these submarines, surface ships and aircraft, which represent the latest achievements of scientific and engineering progress, the talent and skill of scientists and designers, the creative labor of engineers and technicians, the expertise of shipbuilders and aircraft builders and of the makers of weapons and all kinds of military and technological equipment. To get the most out of all this technology and to put it into service is the continuing mission of fleet units, commanding officers and political officers, Party and Komsomol organizations. They are skillfully channeling the productive energy and enthusiasm of all our personnel into a unified effort and are motivating them to achieve their objective as rapidly as possible.

As they study modern military technology and ordnance and acquire solid skills and know-how in using them efficiently under combat conditions involving rapid maneuver and flow over broad expanses of the seas and oceans, our crews are making full use of the rich experience gained from their seafaring and long cruises and of the achievements of Soviet military science. Exemplary performance of combat training tasks and constant upgrading of vigilance and combat readiness—this is the response of our Navymen to the concern of the Party and the Government for the USSR Armed Forces.

The growth and combat readiness of our Navy are a warning to those militaristic circles of imperialism which continue to oppose the lessening of tension in the world, intensify the arms race, make preparations for war, and create more and more dangerous flash points in various parts of the world.

These advocates of militaristic preparations are motivated primarily by their hatred of socialism and their anxiety to achieve military supremacy over it. The world has never known such a dangerous, reckless arms race that now is being engaged in by the United States. In the past ten years they have doubled their military expenditures, and by 1985 they plan to spend more than 250 billion dollars for these purposes, following the Pentagon line.

Most of this money will flow into the coffers of concerns which manufacture mobile-based MX intercontinental ballistic missiles, Trident-system nuclear submarines and missiles for them, warships of various types including nuclear-powered aircraft carriers, and combat aircraft.

In intensifying the arms race, the USA is also demanding increased effort from her allies. Under pressure from Washington, most of the NATO nations are increasing their expenditures. Many of them are carrying out large-scale plans for building up and modernizing their armaments and armed forces.

The annual 3% increase in actual military expenditures by the NATO countries and the decision to manufacture and deploy in Western Europe medium-range nuclear missiles are in pursuit of one basic objective—to change the strategic situation, giving a lop-sided advantage to the nations participating in NATO. Their political leaders are making propaganda about the possibility of "partial" or "limited" employment of nuclear weapons, and this is leading inevitably to a further increase in the danger of unlimited nuclear war.

One concentrated manifestation of the North Atlantic bloc's preparations for war was the series of maneuvers performed by their armed forces in the autumn of 1980, which were held under the code name AUTUMN FORGE-80. Participating in these exercises were more than 300,000 servicemen, thousands of tanks and aircraft, and 220 combat ships. Although this was not the first year in which such maneuvers had been held, many things were practiced for the first time: the employment of civilian aviation to transport troops, the landing of troops directly on a "battlefield," and others.

The scale of the AUTUMN FORGE-80 maneuvers, in itself, indicates the aggressive nature of the basic political aims of the NATO leaders. The architects of these militaristic demonstrations make no secret of the fact that they are directed against the socialist countries. But those responsible for this wasteful militaristic show should always remember that the constructive labor of the Soviet people and their fellow socialist peoples and our great revolutionary achievements are under reliable protection. V. I. Lenin taught us to be constantly on the alert; our history teaches us this also, and it derives from the characteristics of the international situation.

The Communist Party and the Soviet people are devoting the proper attention to strengthening our country's defense capacity and are seeing to it that our Armed Forces have the necessary means at their disposal to perform their responsible mission—to be the guardian of our people's labor and the bulwark of world peace. "Our valiant Armed Forces," declared Comrade L. I. Brezhnev, General Secretary of the Central Committee of the CPSU and Chairman of the Presidium of the Supreme Soviet of the USSR, in a speech at Alma-Ata on 29 August 1980, "have at their disposal everything necessary to repel any aggressor." We shall always be able to defend our rights and our legitimate interests.

Always remembering their military duty and their responsibility to our Homeland, our Navymen have come to the 26th CPSU Congress with high marks in military and political training and in upgrading combat readiness, and they are glad to report to our Party's forum their firm resolve to devote all their efforts to further strengthening the security of the Soviet nation.

The question of how to strengthen the firepower and upgrade the combat readiness of the Navy has always been and still remains uppermost in the minds of the leaders of our fleets.

Our combat training during the past year has been conducted in a well organized, goal-oriented fashion; its intensity has been somewhat increased, and the volume and complexity of the tasks practiced has also been increased. We consider the state of combat training in the fleets to be one of the most important components of combat readiness.

Careful study and analysis of results in navigation and in the employment of ordnance and equipment during combat training have made it possible to correct some articles of our tactical doctrine and to work out practical recommendations for increasing the operational efficiency of ships, ordnance and equipment and for developing the theory and practice of warfare at sea.

The tactical exercises conducted in the fleets and the maneuvers, missile launches and gunnery drills performed have verified the improvement in our personnel's level of skill. Qualitative indices in the employment of all types of ordnance remain steady at a high level; and our combat exercises are being performed in conjunction with tactical missions, under geographical and weather conditions characteristic of the theaters involved.

Analyzing the results of military and political training on the eve of the 26th Party Congress, we can report that the overwhelming majority of our officers, admirals and generals possess excellent practical skills and are capable of operating competently the sophisticated equipment of armed conflict at sea. Their professional and methodological training has been improved.

Commanding officers, political organs, staffs and Party and Komsomol organizations in the fleets are working hard to develop in all servicemen strong ideological conviction and political vigilance, and to motivate their personnel to salute the 26th CPSU Congress in worthy fashion. Ideological work in the fleets has been enriched with new content; it is different both in its essence and in the variety of its forms. This has been facilitated to a considerable degree by the implementation of some recommendations made by a conference of Army and Navy command and political personnel and ideological workers which took place during the past year. More attention is being devoted to exposure of bourgeois propaganda, Zionism and Maoism and to the inculcation of class hatred for the enemies of our Homeland.

The personnel of the Navy have responded positively to the resolution of the Central Committee of the CPSU "on socialist competition in saluting appropriately the 26th CPSU Congress." Our principal efforts in the organization of competition within the fleets have been directed toward efficient performance by the personnel of ships and aviation and infantry units of specific tasks in their military and political training, complete and high-quality execution of plans, efficiency in the instruction process, top-quality military skill, further strengthening of military discipline, teamwork within units, and increasing vigilance and combat readiness.

The Navy's Communists understand that success in any activity is ensured by good organization at duty stations.

Therefore in the fleets some specific measures have been planned and carried out to facilitate and promote the development of initiative in individual seamen and small units, wide propagation of patriotic endeavors, and the sharing of instructive experience in the organization of pre-Congress socialist competition. All this has helped us to discover and bring into play some previously unutilized reserves.

Well thought out and coordinated organizational work by military soviets, commanding officers, political officers, Party and Komsomol organizations designed to involve all personnel of ships and units in pre-Congress socialist competition and to ensure its broad scope and high efficiency, made it possible to fulfill the socialist obligations which had been assumed.

Commanding officers, staffs and political organs on the whole were able to make effective use of socialist competition in the interests of high-quality performance of military and political training tasks. Assumed socialist obligations were successfully discharged by the initiators of competition in the Navy—the large ASW ship *Petropavlovsk* of the Pacific Fleet and the submarine force of the Northern Fleet. Their performance and that of other aviation and infantry units, ships and departments which excelled in pre-Congress socialist competition served as an example for all; and making this available to the personnel of all ships and units means creating one of the important conditions for further strengthening combat readiness of our naval forces.

All this is our active contribution, the steps we have taken to increase the actual combat readiness of the Navy; and only by steadily consolidating our gains and by skillfully developing in the future the results achieved can we ensure the necessary forward movement in increasing the combat power of the fleet.

In reporting our progress to the Party Congress, we must not overlook those tasks which still remain to be accomplished in the future.

Our principal efforts should be concentrated on the further upgrading of combat readiness. We need to develop in our officers, admirals and generals broad operational-tactical knowledge, organizational ability and skill in handling firmly the forces under their control. In training the commanders of ships, units and forces of the fleet, we must always remember that operational-tactical training has been, is now, and will remain the most important element. This must be directed toward increasing the efficiency with which all forces and means available are employed, and toward the development and practical application of those means and procedures which permit maximal utilization of the fighting qualities inherent in today's ships, aircraft, ordnance and technological equipment. It is precisely in this area that we see great possibilities for further upgrading the combat readiness of our fleet. The tactical training of officers at all echelons must be a crucial factor in the evaluation of the combat skill of both these officers themselves and the personnel of their ships and units.

In the performance of any combat exercise, commanding officers must learn to combine maneuver skillfully with competent tactical employment of ordnance. A combat exercise cannot be carried out for the sole purpose of making a good mark in gunnery, for if such is the case, an insufficiently objective evaluation of tactical elements will inevitably lead to stereotyping and lack of initiative in actions at sea. In the tactical training of commanding officers, the instructional material base should be more intensively utilized. The use of instructional technology [trainers] for training commanding officers and staffs in the combat employment of ordnance and in operations and tactics, simulating the complex conditions under which naval combat is conducted today, must be practiced as extensively as possible.

One of the indices of combat readiness is the good operating condition of ordnance and equipment and the availability of well-trained teams and crews. But this depends, in the first instance, on good specialty training. Every commanding officer, in determining the degree of his ship's combat readiness, must realize clearly that it is primarily the good operating condition and readiness of his ship and her ordnance and equipment which constitutes the material basis for success in combat.

Constant close attention must be paid to operational reliability, to timely and efficient implementation of planning and of prophylactic inspection and maintenance, to the performance of regulatory operations at frequent intervals with the least possible expenditure of labor and materials, and to the search for new, economical operating regimes for ordnance and equipment.

Matters involving the strengthening of military discipline comprise an important aspect of our activity. Every commanding officer, political officer, Party and Komsomol activist must thoroughly understand that success will come to the person who insists strictly and persistently on military discipline and on absolute compliance with regulations. Here and there, however, there are officers who are still slowly restructuring their personal approach to the strengthening of discipline. Some commanding officers, political organs and staffs try to solve the problem of military discipline with general pronouncements and ineffective measures, without addressing the individual department, unit or ship.

We must increase the concreteness of political education work and inculcate in personnel an understanding of their special, personal responsibility for combat readiness and for intelligent, persevering performance in any job.

Ideological work must be made as businesslike, concrete, thorough and efficient as possible; the main thing is to strive for effective unity of word and deed, as called for by the resolution of the Central Committee of the CPSU "on the further improvement of ideological and political-education work" in the June and October (1980) Plenums of the Party's Central Committee.

Henceforth we must understand the role of socialist competition in the performance of military and political training tasks and in strengthening military discipline. We must get rid of formalism, teach commanding officers and political workers how to organize competition, and strive to make it inject competitive spirit into military training in practical ways, so that all will strive to achieve the highest scores in combat training activities. Socialist obligations must be discharged by all personnel and must be realized in their daily lives.

All future organizational and political education work must be conditioned by a thorough study and practical realization of the decisions of the 26th Party Congress. We must strengthen and solidify the political and moral state of our people, rally them around the Party's Central Committee, and instill in them readiness to stand up for our country and to defend her national interests.

The unity and solidarity of the Navy's Communists in their support of the Central Committee of the CPSU were demonstrated in the recent meetings and elections within our Party organizations. Those which took place on the eve of the 26th Party Congress were noteworthy for their high-principled tone, their businesslike atmosphere, their self-critical approach to their own work, and the striving of these Communists to discharge their pre-Congress obligations with high marks.

Navymen, like all Soviet people, have responded with tremendous interest and warm approval to the plan of the Central Committee of the CPSU for the 26th Party Congress: "Principal directions of USSR economic and social development for the years 1981 to 1985 and for the period up to 1990," published in the press for general discussion by all our people.

The magnificent prospects for the economic and social development of our Homeland evoke in every serviceman a feeling of profound satisfaction and a burning desire to do even better at his own job, in order to increase still more his own contribution to the strengthening of the Homeland's economic and defense capacity.

Preparation for the 26th CFSU Congress, which has evoked a new upsurge of creative activity on the part of all personnel, has laid a new foundation for improving the efficiency and quality of combat training and for extensively propagating outstanding, instructive experience.

The intensity of combat training continues to increase. Having begun the training year in the military and political training system, many ships, units and forces are successfully carrying out the tasks planned for them in the winter period. Ship and aircraft crews, staffs and commanding officers are striving to make the most productive use of the time allotted, in order to get the best possible results in tactical exercises, practice attacks and combat exercises.

The crew of the Red Banner Northern Fleet SSBN which is commanded by Captain 1st Rank G. Nikitin has come up with an initiative in socialist competition to follow the lead of the large ASW ship *Petropavlovsk* and has issued a challenge to all Navy personnel to achieve an increase in combat readiness and a strengthening of regulation procedure, and has set for 1981 some new and higher goals.

This challenge has been accepted by other fleet units. Navymen are approaching the 26th Party Congress with high marks in military and political training, vigilantly standing watch at sea, increasing even more persistently the efficiency and quality of training, and upgrading organization and regulation procedure; they understand clearly how responsible they are for discharging the obligations they have assumed in honor of the Congress.

It is a point of honor with Navy personnel to make the current combat training year a year of successful performance of all tasks, a year of attainment of the highest goals in mastering today's combat technology and all methods and forms of armed conflict.

Navymen are well aware that actual realization of the enormous tasks of communist construction will demand of them great creative effort, self-sacrificing military labor, faultless performance of military duty, and exemplary service to the Homeland. They are ready to report to the 26th Congress of the Communist Party that they will devote all their efforts and knowledge to strengthening the defensive power of our Homeland.

CHAPTER THREE

Science

What follows is the shortest article in this collection, but it earns its place through succinct clarity. In much of his writing Sergei Gorshkov, in keeping with the Soviet doctrine of the time, separated naval science from naval art. He saw art, which is addressed in the next chapter, as the individual, inspirational, creative style of military problem solving; it is innate in leadership and our ability to employ military means innovatively and imaginatively. Science, the subject of this chapter, was more earthy, a "system of knowledge," and referred to a collective, methodological approach necessary to the understanding of capabilities and numbers, tactics and technology. To employ the art of our profession, we must know the science that underpins it.

Gorshkov believed that to be scientifically credible, a fleet must be a balanced system. Such balance is the goal of the majority if not all ambitious sea powers in the twenty-first century and comes, quite obviously, at a cost. Gorshkov meant that the fleet must be able to carry out a wide range of missions precisely because of its varied composition. It needed to be an optimum mix of surface, submarine, and aviation elements, all working together, with the whole delivering more than the sum of its parts. There is no doubt that both East and West were riding a wave of technological advancement in the 1960s and, as history shows us, Gorshkov's transformation of the Soviet navy from coastal defense force to oceangoing, globally active fleet was largely accomplished by the middle of that decade. In a later work he claimed that the transformation was realized through a technical revolution in military affairs, a concept that has become familiar to all naval powers.[1] But there was more. Soviet out-of-area deployments and visits quadrupled in number between 1965 and 1968 and had more than doubled again by 1974.[2] If there was science, it was applied in construction, technology, tactics, and deployment cycles.

However, the Soviet navy was then, as it would be for the remainder of the Cold War, divided into four home fleets: the Northern, sailing out of Severomorsk; the Pacific, based in Vladivostok; the Baltic in Kaliningrad; and the Black Sea Fleet in Sevastopol. The balance that Gorshkov sought may have been achieved across the entirety of his navy, but it was not necessarily true within each of the distinctive fleet groupings. Is this important? The geography of the Soviet Union meant that the nearly landlocked Baltic and Black Sea Fleets were configured for asserting local sea control and supporting the Red Army in its ground operations. They did not, for instance, include ballistic missile submarines in their inventory. The Northern and Pacific Fleets, on the other hand, were structured for aerial reconnaissance and long-range strategic strike but were comparatively unconvincing in their amphibious capability. To the scientific ingredient of fleet composition must be added, therefore, the corresponding factor of disposition. Geographically smaller countries may well choose for practical and geostrategic purposes to divide their fleets into different centers of excellence, fitted for the role they are most likely to fulfill. The UK's Royal Navy is a case in point, with submarines based in Scotland, amphibious ships in Plymouth, and carriers and air defense destroyers sailing out of Portsmouth. But when vast continental or oceanic distances are involved, as they were for the Soviet Union and still are for Russia and the United States today, any prospect of mutual support may be lost as the discrete and distinct fleets develop separately, potentially adopting differing tactics and perspectives.

Nonetheless, Gorshkov's achievement was palpable. New classes of ship were being introduced and build rates, in terms of hull numbers at least, outpaced the West. In his writing he made much of the importance of the "material-technical base" of the fleet, of new weapons systems, and, in particular, nuclear missiles. However, closing the gap between the systems' capabilities and the tactics for employing them received particular attention in this 1967 article. Tactics, to Gorshkov, were not only the most manifest application of naval science, the front line of doctrine, but also the most versatile. Whereas platforms and weapons systems were years in the making, tactics could be changed in an instant and thus naval science was always an ongoing endeavor. Testing, exercising, and combat training built on the material-technical base and resulted in incremental improvement; one might then assume that they gave launch to the "art" of the naval commander.

Today, the issue of naval "science" is of no lesser importance. As new technologies are introduced, from unmanned platforms and fifth-generation fighters to cyber capabilities unrestricted by any physical boundary, they affect the "balance" of the fleet. Do they complement or replace existing force structures? Do our tactics reflect their presence? Indeed, what, in the twenty-first century, is the purpose of a warship? Gorshkov's writing helps to address these questions by reminding us that, first and foremost, we must understand what is at our disposal, learn to work with it, and then constantly test and adjust to make improvements. A great artist cannot begin to create a masterpiece until he has fully come to terms with the materials he is going to use.

THE DEVELOPMENT OF SOVIET NAVAL SCIENCE

Morskoy Sbornik, 1967

In the mid-1950s, in connection with the revolution in military affairs, the Central Committee of our Party defined the path of fleet development, as well as the fleet's role and place in the system of Armed Forces in the country. The course taken was one which required the construction of an oceangoing fleet, capable of carrying out offensive strategic missions. Submarines and naval aviation, equipped with nuclear weapons, had a leading place in the program. Thus, there began a new stage in the development of the fleet and of its naval science.

Realization of the latest achievements in science and production, and the creation, on this base, of what were, in principle, new weapons for the armed struggle made it possible, in a short period, to bring about a radical change in the technical base, and, in essence, to create a qualitatively new type of Armed Force, our oceangoing fleet, in which submarine forces, aviation, surface warships, and other types of forces developed harmoniously. This was the authorized source for the creation of a balanced Navy, capable of successfully conducting combat operations under different circumstances. (By a well-balanced fleet we mean a fleet which, in composition and armament, is capable of carrying out missions assigned to it, not only in a nuclear war, but in a war which does not make use of nuclear weapons, and is also able to support state interests at sea in peacetime.)

For the first time in its history our Navy was converted, in the full sense of the word, into an offensive type of long-range armed force. Along with the Strategic Rocket Forces the Navy had become the most important weapon the Supreme Command had, one which could exert a decisive influence in the course of an armed struggle on theaters of military operations of vast extent.

Now our fleet has colossal operational and strategic capabilities, which can in no way be compared with the capabilities of any fleet of the

Sergei Georgiyevich Gorshkov, "The Development of Soviet Naval Science," *Morskoy Sbornik,* no. 2 (February 1967), pp. 20–21.

pre-nuclear epoch, no matter how powerful. But this potential must be brought to bear in full measure in the struggle with a strong naval enemy. It is to precisely this requirement that the development of naval science has been subordinated in recent years.

The fleet, which for a long time could carry on combat operations in seas directly next to its own coasts, and which had had experience in a continental war, carrying out primarily tactical-operational missions, mainly in coordination with ground forces, now sailed the broad expanses of the oceans, and acquired the capacity to carry out strategic missions in the struggle with the strongest of naval enemies. This brought about a fleet requirement for new tactics, for new operational art, and for a theory covering the strategic utilization of its forces.

Initially, when the first models of new combat equipment made their appearance in the fleet arsenal, our scientific thought attempted to use those provisions of the operational art and tactics which they already had, adapting them to the new conditions. But this transition period in the development of naval science was extremely short. The more new weapons for the armed struggle the fleet received, mastering them quickly during intensive combat training, the more clearly the fleet felt the need to develop principally new means and methods for the combat utilization of its forces, the more fully the changes taking place in the fleet's material-technical base were considered, and, consequently, the better they responded to the requirements of nuclear war. The budding revolution in military affairs has now spread to all fields of naval science as well. Useful conclusions were arrived at in the course of breaking down obsolete views and notions, in the course of active and bold scientific searching for ways and methods of using what were, in principle, new fleet forces and weapons in combat, and in the process of critical analysis of the established theory of naval science, of the experience of the armed struggle and of combat training available to our fleet. Quite a few, original, and extremely effective methods for conducting the armed struggle with a powerful naval enemy were found.

The first thing to occur was the liquidation of the gap existing between the combat capabilities of weapons and the tactics of using them in combat. The theory of naval science was freed of its clearly obsolete conceptions, and was completely reoriented to support the practical requirements of the fleets in carrying out strategic and tactical-operational missions corresponding to the new combat capabilities.

All branches of naval science began to use the new methods of operations research, based on the use of electronic computer techniques. The use of these methods has considerably accelerated scientific research and pursuits, and has made it possible to create a contemporary theory for the operational art, and for naval tactics, which responds quickly to present day requirements of the armed struggle.

Grounded on the new material-technical base, the theory of operational utilization of fleet forces gives full consideration to the increase in the fleet's role in attaining the strategic goals of the struggle at sea with a powerful enemy, as well as to the capability the fleet has attained for direct combat operations against enemy bases and territory over vast distances.

Contemporary naval tactics—the most mobile and flexible branch of naval science—have at their disposal a vast arsenal of methods and means for carrying out the various types of missions in different situations. They provide for the use of submarines carrying missiles and torpedoes, strike aviation, surface warships of various classes, units of naval infantry, and other types of fleet forces on independent operations, as well as jointly with other branches of the Armed Forces.

With the growth in the economic might of the Soviet Union have come ever expanding interests in the seas and oceans; so new requirements have been imposed on the Navy to protect those interests against the encroachments of the imperialists.

Soviet naval science, which is based on a uniquely scientific methodological base, that of dialectical materialism, is completely respondent to the fleet's material-technical base, and provides for its requirements in contemporary methods of struggle in a nuclear missile war, in carrying out the missions and protecting the state interests of the USSR on the seas and oceans. All of these means and methods of the armed struggle are regularly checked out in the course of combat training, are refined and concretized by virtue of mastering new equipment, and are enriched by the experience gained from using weapons on fleet maneuvers and exercises.

Soviet naval science is under constant development. Every new discovery increases the capabilities of our state to strengthen defensive capabilities, but inevitably poses new problems for naval science, creative development of which by the shortest possible route will lead to a further increase in the combat readiness and might of the fleet. And this continuing process will go on at an ever increasing tempo.

Navymen have a clear picture of the primary requirement of the present day, that of maintaining all branches of naval science at the level of the latest achievements of science and technology, in condition to provide for the complete realization of all combat possibilities incorporated in the latest models of weapons and their delivery systems. Navymen see their responsible and honorable mission as one of providing for unity of theory and practice, of untiring seeking for new, ever more modern forms and methods of carrying on combat operations at sea.

CHAPTER FOUR

Art

If Gorshkov's "science" was methodological, his "art" was innate. In his scientific approach, which combined technology with tactics, repeating the same action in the same circumstances logically meant getting the same results time and again. The art of the naval commander was different. To Gorshkov art was in the commander's appreciation of history, his judgment, and his ability to adapt quickly to the circumstances he faced. If science was tactics, art was strategy. In principle, the two approaches should be combined, meaning that a major component of the artistry of the great commander was the ability to know how, where, and when to apply the science.

In *The Sea Power of the State* Gorshkov addressed what he described as the problems of naval art. It is a lengthy but well-structured discussion that draws the reader into the author's way of thinking. He began by acknowledging the closeness of naval art to its military equivalent, but then pointed out the differences between sea and land warfare. Whereas armies fight other armies, he observed, navies not only fight other navies but they also fight against the shore.

At first reading this may appear to be an obvious and rather crude distinction but its elemental root is worthy of consideration. It highlights an inherent jointness in the maritime environment that is absent elsewhere—operations are never constrained exclusively to the sea. Gorshkov noted that even the most brilliant military commander is often ignorant of anything beyond his immediate domain (Napoleon's land-centricity comes in for criticism, for example) but in contrast the naval commander must be the master of more; he must appreciate combat at, on, under, over, and most of all *from* the sea. Gorshkov's discussion of the dilemma of "fleet against fleet" and "fleet against shore" raises once again the familiar theme of balanced fleets and leads to wider questions on the importance of littoral maneuver and economic warfare. His words, therefore, are prescient when later, post–Cold War, Western maritime strategies, including those that prioritize global systemic protection, are considered.

Despite being credited with building an oceangoing fleet, Gorshkov never attempted to claim that war at sea was preeminent. He made plain that he believed that the outcome of any war would be settled by "decisive objectives" on land and, consequently, that fleet-versus-fleet actions were unlikely to ever be the most important factor. His writing returned several times to the successes of major blue-water actions and their importance to wider war efforts and he was especially fond of referring to World War II in the Pacific. There, he stated, the major engagements between the American and Japanese navies may appear to have been in the form of fleet against fleet, but their true purpose was always linked to the shore. The judgment of the naval commander and, especially, his appreciation of and ability to calculate risk, was also high on Gorshkov's agenda. As a scholar of the Pacific campaign one might assume that he admired Chester Nimitz's famous 1942 instruction on the subject. On the eve of the Battle of Midway Nimitz signaled his interpretation of "calculated risk," which he took to mean the avoidance of exposure to attack by the enemy without good prospect of inflicting greater damage in return.[1]

Once he had outlined his thoughts on the imperative issue of the purpose of a navy, Gorshkov tackled a series of supplementary questions. Twenty-first-century doctrinal publications and academic literature is awash with theoretical constructs through which to consider military problems—the principles of war, for instance, or the staff/war college estimate process. In *The Sea Power of the State* Gorshkov offered his own approach, tailored specifically for the challenges of naval art: it included the scope of the conflict (i.e., whether it was local, regional, or global), the importance of strike, the evolution of battle, the interaction of the weapons, sensors, platforms, and other forces involved, maneuver, speed, time, and dominance at sea—all needed to be considered by the naval commander.

In its time, and certainly after its downfall, the USSR became associated with a "quantity before quality" approach to warfare, but Gorshkov made an eloquent case for technological superiority over mere numbers. *Strike*, to him, would be of increasing importance, and part of a commander's art was to recognize how to turn tactical actions—the single strike—into strategic outcomes. Today's precision strike weapons such as long-range, sea-launched land attack missiles justify his reasoning. The ability to transition between the land, maritime, and air domains was an integral part of *battle*; but to the physical, terrestrial environments of the 1960s, the twenty-first century could add the electromagnetic spectrum, cyberspace, and space. The modern commander must be able to roll seamlessly between them all.

Maneuver was about orders of magnitude and scale, driving the requirement not just for weapon carriers but increasingly for intelligence, surveillance, and reconnaissance (ISR) platforms, too. Little has changed; there is always a race to achieve the best possible "picture." Closely connected, his words on *speed* showed that Gorshkov was convinced that future conflict would be characterized more by short, sharp, hit-and-run engagements than by attrition—a lesson that has arguably been re-learned by this century's state and non-state actors alike. *Time* is discussed not simply as a measure of duration of presence or control, but in terms reminiscent of what has since become known as time-sensitive targeting. And finally, Gorshkov denoted *dominance at sea* as a "special category" solely for maritime conflict; here, the author followed the Anglo-American school of thought but, in a return to political rhetoric, disassociated the Soviet Union from the imperialism and quest for world dominance he saw in the West. Instead he saw dominance in the maritime environment as an enabling function, supporting a full-spectrum approach across all environments.

Arguably, twenty-first-century commanders and strategists have often been led by technology, fitting their plans and concepts around their precision weapons and advanced ISR rather than fitting those systems into their plans. The result can be a tactical hit but strategic miss. However, times are changing and the decade-long Western experience of campaigning has taught commanders the value of painting the whole canvas, not just one part of it. Some may still doubt any distinction between science and art in contemporary warfare, but in the 1970s Gorshkov had no such qualms; he laid out a framework of characteristics of naval art not to be dismissed, either then or now. Those characteristics are as relevant today as any other instrument in the modern commander's arsenal, ready to be consulted when the situation requires, or improved upon as the artist's own ideas form.

PROBLEMS OF NAVAL ART

The Sea Power of the State, 1979

Naval art is a historical category, since each period of history has its own theory and practice of armed conflict at sea suitably reflecting the point reached in the development of material means for such a conflict.

In the course of the centuries old history of navies, naval art has developed unevenly. It has known smooth, gradual movements ahead and tempestuous surges, raising it to a height previously appearing unattainable. Periods of decline mostly coincided with a strengthening of reaction and the stagnation of economic and political life. Flourishing periods usually corresponded to revolutionary events in the life of nations. Such was, for example, the radical change in military affairs associated with the victory

---

Sergei Georgiyevich Gorshkov, "Problems of Naval Art," *The Sea Power of the State* (Annapolis: Naval Institute Press, 1979): 223–34.

of the Great October Socialist Revolution which opened a broad path to creativity of the popular masses, cleared the way for great revolutionary transformations in military matters necessary to the young socialist state for the struggle against the imperialists, seeking to take from the people the power they had gained.

Naval art, like any other scientific theory, is intimately connected with practice, and rests on the lessons from past wars and the many-sided experience of operational and combat training conducted in peacetime. Practice is a criterion of the truth. Without study of the experience of past wars and its critical application, the development of naval art cannot be ensured. Study of historical experience on the basis of dialectical materialism is a method of grasping the patterns of armed struggle at sea, the laws, lines and directions of the development of naval art.

The development of naval art is closely tied to the development of military art, despite the fact that for all the identity of the goals of land forces and navies, the tasks and modes of their operation, determined by the medium and means of struggle, substantially differ.

Fleet Against Fleet and Fleet Against Shore

The main task of land forces, as is known, has always been the destruction of the opposing foe in order to take over his territories and possessions. In a given case the tasks of the operations of land forces in the purely military sense might be figuratively expressed by the phrase 'soldier against soldier.' This is not so in the sphere of the navy. As well as the tasks of fighting an enemy fleet, it is also faced with tasks associated with the operations against territories and groupings of troops therein. Thus, the formula 'soldier against soldier,' translated into terms of the fleet, takes on the form 'fleet against fleet and fleet against shore.'

The correlation of these two tasks throughout history has naturally not always been constant. Among the operations of fleet against fleet one may include battles and operations to destroy the ships of the enemy at sea and in the bases, and the struggle on oceanic and sea communications (disruption, defense). A vivid example of this is provided by the campaigns, sea operations and battles of the First World War, in the course of which the fleets acted little against the shore. But history also provides many examples of active operations of the fleet against the shore.

Traditional were the staging of sea landings of varying size and the delivery of strikes of ship armament on targets located on shore. The new models of operations of a fleet against the shore consist in delivering a strike of carrier aviation on ground targets and groupings of troops, and in the destruction by nuclear missile strikes from submarines of land targets of great strategic and economic importance.

Since the goals of a war were achieved mostly by taking over the territory of the enemy, successful operations of a fleet against the shore brought a better result than the operations of fleet against fleet. In the first case the fleet solved a direct "territorial" task, whereas in the second, victory over the enemy's fleet merely created the pre-requisites for the later solution of territorial tasks.

True, such pre-requisites in individual cases were of paramount importance as compared with the actions of land forces connected with them. For example, the defeat by the English navy of the so-called invincible Spanish Armada in the Atlantic Ocean completely excluded the possibility of invasion of the territory of England by Spanish land troops. The defeat of the French squadron at Aboukir Bay already mentioned, pre-determined the failure of the Napoleonic squadrons in the Greater Antilles Islands and the Philippines in fact decided the fate of the territorial claims of the Americans and the outcome of the Spanish-American War.

The decisive and active operations of the Soviet navy in the sea theaters in the period of the Great Patriotic War forced the German command to abandon completely attempts to use their fleet against Soviet land forces and the capture of territory from the sea directions, even when they had the strategic initiative.

Let us take a closer look at the relationship of these two main directions in the combat activity of navies.

The final results of the operations of a fleet against an enemy fleet have been achieved by different methods, determined by the material-technical base at the disposal of the fleets in a particular period of history.

Characteristic of the fleets of antiquity was the clash of a mass of vessels passing into a disordered tussle, as the victor of which emerged the fleet with the larger complement and possessing ships of greater strength than the enemy. In the age of sailing fleets, this struggle had the character of rivalry between comparatively small squadrons of battleships in mutual display on extensive sea expanses and occupation of a more advantageous

position for maneuver and use of one's own weapons. Ever greater importance was assumed by the combination of maneuver and fire-power of the
battle forces, representing the highest concentration of strike power of the
fleet against similar forces of the enemy. This aspect of the operations of
essentially homogenous forces also persisted in the initial stage of development of steam fleets, the principles of the use of which differed little from
those adopted in sailing fleets.

As fleets developed, with formation of diverse forces (submarine and
aircraft) and also the widening of the arsenal of naval weapons (guns, torpedoes and mines), the opposition of fleets at sea assumed ever new features. The gun duels of different ships were augmented by attacks of light,
rapid, non-armored torpedo forces, submarines and aircraft. The operations of fleet against fleet therefore required great diversity in planning.
Sea tactics began to look at battles of diverse forces with their wide interaction in combination with major defense measures and other forms of
maintenance. The appearance of rocket weapons accentuated this tendency. Its latest expression is the fight against weapons which assumed
almost the same importance as the destruction of ships—carriers of these
weapons. In individual cases it may become the sole means of ship defense.

The evolution of forms of combat operations of the fleet helps to define
the tendency towards a further complication of this process.

The use of missiles with nuclear warheads, for example, generates
major and complex problems associated with the appraisal of the balance
of forces in the operation of fleet against fleet at sea and in protection of its
forces.

Now the criterion of comparability of the potential of fleets is the ratio
of their overall combat power in different combinations of diverse forces
and resources for different variants of a situation. An objective approach
to the determination of fighting power of the forces of the fleet helps to
determine a necessary and sufficient composition of forces in the most
rational combination, which we called balanced.

Analysis of sea engagements, battles and operations suggests that
despite very decisive operations in counterposing the forces of the fleets,
their results, as a rule, were no more than operational. Some exceptions
are, for example, the results of the sea engagements in the 1898 Spanish-
American War, the 1904–05 Russo-Japanese War and also the attack of
the Japanese fleet on Pearl Harbor in December 1941. At the same time

the totality of the operations of a fleet against an enemy fleet in war was often of strategic importance. Thus, for example, of undoubted strategic importance were the sea campaigns of the Russian fleet in the Mediterranean in the eighteenth to nineteenth centuries, the struggle for Atlantic communications in the First and Second World War in the sea theaters adjoining our territory. Should world imperialism launch a new world war the prevention of nuclear strikes from the sea would be undoubtedly of a strategic character.

An important feature of the forces of a fleet in operations against an enemy fleet is their relatively greater independence than in operations against the shore. This is largely determined by the fact that the operations of fleet against fleet occur predominantly in areas of the seas and oceans distant from the coast, where the forces of the navy can in the main fulfill their combat tasks. In this sphere the fleet makes fullest use of such qualities as high readiness for immediate action, mobility, ability to be at sea for a long time and wage a battle with the enemy fleet a long way from the areas of its permanent home. The realization of such qualities, as indicated by numerous examples from wars of the past has always given advantages to that side which has been able to combine and use them for achieving the goals of war.

The tendency now taking shape towards a mutual interlinking of the spheres of combat operations by branches of the armed forces, due to the development of military technology, introduces certain corrections into this thesis. However, at the present time too the fleet has a leading role in the fight against an enemy fleet.

The operations of fleet against fleet encompass the extensive field of the operational and strategic use of this branch of the armed forces in sea and oceanic theaters. Such use of the fleet may be regarded as a bitter struggle waged in two main directions.

The first is based on operations of the forces of fleet against fleet in pure form, i.e., not directly connected with the simultaneous solution of other tasks, either in sea or continental theaters.

The hub of these operations in the past was the fight of the main forces of the fleets of the adversaries against one another with the aim of gaining dominance at sea and seizing and keeping the strategic initiatives in the theater to ensure the solution of the next tasks stemming from the aims of the war or campaign.

In the epoch of sailing fleets these were general engagements of the battle forces. Later, steam fleets tended to conduct such engagements according to established tradition, right up to the end of the First World War. The last such engagement was at Jutland. The final result of this engagement was totally unlike what each of the opposing sides wanted to see. This expressed the objective pattern of the development of the fleets and naval art, consisting in the fact that general engagements which before could materially change the situation at sea in favor of one of the belligerents not only lost their importance but became practically unrealistic. At the same time the sphere of use of the main strike forces of the fleets for taking on equals, in the hope of gaining dominance at sea, narrowed. There was an ever stronger tendency, becoming paramount in the course of the Second World War, for the general scope of operations of the forces of fleet against fleet through successive and simultaneous operations and battles in different directions or theaters to increase, both independently and in interaction with other branches of the armed forces.

Examples of this may be afforded by the operations of part of the forces of the English fleet in destroying the grouping of ships of the Italian fleet at Taranto. As a result of this operation, the British in fact gained dominance in the Mediterranean, but could not retain it in the course of the war. They ended up in a difficult position after a strong grouping of German aviation, specially switched there, developed active operations in the Mediterranean.

One year after the operation in Taranto, the Japanese, using the aircraft-carrying forces of their fleet, struck at the main grouping of the US Navy in Pearl Harbor with the aim of gaining dominance in the Pacific.[1]

Thus, the Second World War, with little exception, did not in fact provide classical examples of the independent operations of fleet against fleet to gain and hold dominance at sea.

The second direction of this form of combat operations of fleet against fleet is provided by actions associated with operations against the shore and also to ensure trans-oceanic or sea communications. Without exaggeration it may be stated that most of the combat clashes of the major

---

1. The Americans lost 18 large ships, of which four battleships were destroyed and four put out of action for a long time.

forces of the opposing fleets in this war took this direction. Thus, the battles off Midway Island and in the Philippines Sea and in the area of Wake Island, Rabaul and Port Moresby and others were a constituent part of sea landing operations in the Pacific. At the same time clearly falling within the category of operations associated with mainstreaming communications are the battles off Cape Matapan, the operations to destroy the German battleship *Bismarck*, and others.

The equipping of the fleets with nuclear missile weapons has now accentuated the manifestation of the tendency for the importance of the operations of fleet against shore to grow.

Analysis of the views of specialists in different countries in the direction of development of the forces and resources of the fleets in the last ten to fifteen years suggests that in modern conditions the role of opposition of the fleets, undertaken to achieve the objectives of other operations, continues to grow. An exception may be operations in theaters limited in size where the possible attempts of one of the opposing sides to attain dominance in a given theater cannot be discounted. Such a course of events may be characteristic of a situation when one of the sides has indisputable superiority in a given specific theater. Here, we have in mind events similar to those which came about in the Gulf of Tonkin during the war against the Vietnamese people, where the American Seventh Fleet, possessing overwhelming superiority in force, sought throughout the war to transform this superiority into dominance at sea in the zone of operations of its main forces.

However, the course and outcome of a major war will be determined by events on a global scale and by decisive objectives, to attain which each of the opposing sides will strive. This will precisely be the idea behind the use of strike forces of the fleets. In other words, all spheres of opposition of the forces of the fleets in modern conditions will be increasingly influenced by the use of ways and means of deploying the forces directly connected with the operations against the shore. The transition of the operations of the forces of the fleet from operational-tactical to a higher strategic level brings these operations into the category of determinant, overriding all others, including those directed at gaining dominance at sea. And while earlier the crux of the efforts of a fleet was directed against the enemy fleet, now the chief goal of a fleet is becoming that of ensuring the fulfillment of all tasks associated with action against enemy ground objectives and the protection of one's territory from the strikes of his fleet.

In speaking of the operations of the fleet against the shore it must be emphasized that they are just as old a form of using the fleet as the operations of fleet against fleet. The most vivid examples are those connected with the "marche-maneuver" of troops across the sea and their landing on hostile territory (invasion force), which have been undertaken by fleets throughout their history.

As far back as the fifth century B.C., in the course of the Greek-Persian Wars, the Persians used their fleet for landing troops in the rear of the Greek army. In the third century B.C., during the so-called Punic Wars, the Romans undertook large landing operations which played a major role in the battle against Carthage.

In a later period, one may mention the numerous landings of the Russian fleet staged on the Swedish coast in 1720–21 in the course of the Northern War, and on the island of Corfu, the Japanese landing on the Liaotung peninsula in 1904, the landing of German Fascist troops in Norway in 1940, the landing operations conducted by the Soviet Navy in the years of the Great Patriotic War and also landings during the Second World War.

The role and significance of landings and the intensity of this form of operations of the fleet have changed in different periods of history. In many cases the emphasis has been on landings in war. For example, Napoleon in his plans to crush England (at a time when the French still had hopes of gaining dominance in the English Channel) envisaged disembarking on the British Isles a strategic invasion force for which was trained the so-called Boulogne expedition which, however, was not undertaken because of the setbacks of the French fleet in the struggle against the Royal Navy. It should be noted that this event is seen by the English and, by following them, other historians to be the outcome of the indisputable superiority of the English fleet and its naval art over the French fleet and the art of its deployment. But the actual causes of the success of the English consisted primarily in that one-sidedness of the strategy of Napoleon which stemmed from his fondness for operations in land theaters and a misreading of the role of the fleet, the neglect of its possibilities in a war and hence inability to use it in a struggle against a maritime opponent, as was England at that time.

This one-sidedness of the strategic thinking of Napoleon was undoubtedly grasped by Napoleon himself, as witness his intention to shift the blame for blunders in the use of the fleet on to his admirals. Therefore, he was evidently not altogether frank when, in connection with the failures of the fleet he wrote to his naval minister: "All the sea expeditions undertaken since I became head of government have always been unsuccessful because the admirals do not see things as they are and have learnt—I do not know how—that one can wage war without risk."[2] (Translated from Russian.)

The trouble was here, of course, not only the admirals and their passivity, although they were distinguished neither by resoluteness nor high fleet command art. When Napoleon needed talented marshals to realize his plans of campaigns on land, he was able to find them in the army. And the fact that the French fleet in the course of these campaigns repeatedly sustained defeats serves as further confirmation of the inability of Napoleon to evaluate in good time the possibilities available to the French fleet and to use it in the struggle against the enemy.

Later, in the course of the Second World War, the Japanese and Americans set much store by landing operations in the Pacific Ocean. It should be noted that the decisive sea engagements of this theater occurred precisely during landing operations. These engagements naturally assumed the form of the operations of fleet against fleet, although their general purpose was the purpose characteristic of operations of fleet against shore.

It must be added that the opening of a second front, that is, the staging of a strategic landing in Europe in the period of the Second World War, due to the successes of the Soviet troops in the fight against the Hitlerites, depended on the ability of the Allied fleet operating successfully against the shore.

At the same time one cannot help noting that in the course of the First World War only five landings were staged and the biggest landing operation undertaken by the English, in an attempt to disembark off the Dardanelles, failed completely.

The operations of the fleet against the shore in the form of landings in the Second World War assumed such wide proportions and were of such

2. Quoted in B. B. Zherve, *The Naval Strategy of Napoleon*, p. 34, Petrograd, 1922 (in Russian).

great importance that they gave rise to a special direction in the development and building of fleets—the creation of numerous transport-landing and disembarking devices. In the period of the war over 600 landings were mounted. These number about nine landings a month or, on average, one landing every three days. In ten major landing operations alone some 1,700,000 men were put ashore. Over 18,000 ships took part in landing operations. It is significant that nearly all the landings were successful. The Soviet navy also widely employed seaborne landings.

It should be noted that landing operations of the fleets in the Second World War were mostly of a tactical and operational character and only individual landings were of strategic importance.[3]

The fleets throughout their history have also made wide use of such a form of operations against the shore as armament strikes on objectives located in the coastal belt. Here we have in mind not the armament preparations conducted in the course of a battle for disembarking an invasion force by specially planned ordnance strikes, the delivery of which exhausted a given combat operation. Such a form was best developed in the period of the Second World War and also in local wars unleashed by the imperialists in the post-war period.

As an example Table 22 gives some data characterizing the operations of the British Navy in naval bombardment of objectives in the coastal belt in the Second World War.

Large forces of the fleet were mustered for gun strikes on shore objectives. The formations set aside for solving this task included battleships, cruisers and destroyers. In the war against Vietnam the Americans for this purpose took out of mothballs and brought into service the battleship *New Jersey*. The groupings of forces operating against the Vietnamese shore in composition were essentially operational and the result achieved by them did not go beyond the limit of tactical. Such operations of the fleet against the shore, as a rule, did not produce the results expected despite the enlistment of considerable forces.

---

3. Among the strategic landings of the Second World War we may include: the landing of the German Fascist troops in Norway in 1940, the Japanese on the Philippine islands in 1941–42, the Anglo-Americans in North Africa in 1942, in Italy in 1943 and in Normandy in 1944, and the Americans in the Philippines in 1944.

The swift development of aviation and shipbuilding brought into being in the course of the Second World War such a new form of use of the forces of the fleet against the shore as the delivery by carrier-based aircraft on the territory and troops of the enemy.

RESULT OF ARMAMENT STRIKES OF THE BRITISH FLEET ON COASTAL BELT OBJECTIVES IN THE SECOND WORLD WAR

Target of strike	Composition of strike grouping of forces	Losses from gun fire
Mers-el-Kebir 3 July 1940	Force H: 2 battleships, 1 battle cruiser, 1 aircraft carrier, 2 light cruisers, 11 destroyers	Battleship *Bretagne* sunk; the battleships *Dunkerque* and *Provence* and one destroyer damaged.
Genoa 9 February 1941	Force H: 2 battleships, 1 aircraft carrier, 1 light cruisers, 10 destroyers	Electrical plant and arms factories badly damaged. Fires and explosions at the base and in the town. No ships in the base.
Tripoli 21 April 1941	The combined Mediterranean Fleet: 3 battleships, 1 aircraft carrier, 4 light cruisers, 13 destroyers, 1 submarine	Three cargo vessels sunk and other ships damaged. Fires, destruction of several buildings.

Note. The attacking forces suffered no losses.

Admittedly, the experience of such operations was limited to the use of aircraft carriers of only three countries—Britain, Japan and the USA. However, it became convincing proof of the desirability of using this form of operation, which led to a considerable expansion of the building of aircraft carriers. While at the start of the Second World War the three countries had respectively seven, six and five carriers, in December 1941, by the start of the war in the Pacific, Britain already has in service twelve carriers, Japan ten and the USA seven. In the war years 221 aircraft-carrying ships were built. By the end of the Second World War the USA had 118 carriers, including twenty strike carriers, that is, capable of attacking not only warships but also enemy ground objectives.

At first, aircraft carriers were regarded only as ships providing fighter cover from air attack for surface forces and cargo vessels. Then on them fell the task of destroying the fighting ships of the enemy at sea and at the bases. Later, carrier aviation operated widely against ground objectives also in the course of landing and anti-landing operations, likewise in operations and combat actions aimed at weakening enemy aviation groupings.

Examples of this are provided by the strikes on the Gilbert, Marshall, Wake and Marcus Islands and on Tokyo in 1942. These raids were carried out under the motto 'hit and run.' Important ground objectives, including naval ones, came under attack in the operations to destroy the forces of the enemy fleet at the bases. The most characteristic examples were British carrier aircraft at Taranto in November 1940 and Japanese carrier aircraft at Pearl Harbor in December 1941.

The operations of aircraft carriers against the shore came into widest use in landing operations when aircraft carriers were used for 'softening up,' subduing the anti-landing defenses of the enemy and giving aid to their troops in solving the tasks on shore after landing. The experience of the Second World War in the use of carrier aviation against ground objectives was widely used by American militarists in local wars, especially for striking at troops, towns, bases, aerodromes and ground communications in the wars against the Korean People's Democratic Republic and the Democratic Republic of Vietnam.

The introduction of nuclear weapons in to the fleets of the great powers considerably widened the sphere of the use of the forces of the fleets against the shore. At first carrier aviation, and then ballistic missiles launched from submarines, determined the enormous possibilities the fleet had to strike at the territory of the enemy. The operations of fleet against shore assumed fundamentally new significance in war as a whole. They constituted an important part of its strategy.

Today, a fleet operating against the shore is able not only to solve the tasks connected with territorial changes but to directly influence the course and even outcome of a war. In this connection the operations of a fleet against the shore have assumed paramount importance in armed conflict at sea, governing the technical policy of building a fleet and the development of naval art. Confirmation of this is that the USA atomic-powered missile submarines are assigned to the strategic forces and all other ships to the general-purpose forces.

The new possibilities of a fleet in operations against the shore and the resulting serious threat from oceanic directions have determined the character of the main efforts of a fleet in the struggle against an enemy fleet. The most important of them has become the use of the forces of the fleet against the naval strategic nuclear systems of the enemy with the aim of disrupting or weakening to the maximum their strikes on ground objectives. Thus, the flight of a fleet against the fleet of an enemy in new conditions since nuclear weapons have appeared has become a secondary task as compared with the operations of a fleet against the shore.

This also changes the significance of the operations of the fleet fulfilling such traditional tasks as disruption of the sea communications of the enemy and protection of one's own. These operations are now the most important constituent part of the efforts of a fleet, aimed at undermining the military-economic potential of the enemy, that is, at solving one of the special tasks arising from the main tasks of a modern fleet in war.

Operations to disrupt and cut off the sea shipments of the enemy, which used to come directly into the sphere of use of a fleet against an enemy fleet, are now assuming a new direction. Forming part of the general system of operations of a fleet against the shore, they are accentuating the special function of a fleet which it has acquired thanks to modern means of combat—the ability to fulfill strategic tasks of an offensive character by directly acting on the sources of the enemy's military power.

Thus, the traditional operations of fleet against fleet which, since ancient times, have been characteristic of the struggle against sea communications of the opposing sides, are now used in a new, decisive sphere—operations of a fleet against the shore. This trend in the operational and strategic use of the fleet is becoming increasingly prominent and assuming the features of the main field of operations of a fleet, governing all others at all operational levels.

Some Theoretical Problems of Naval Art

Naval art and the ways of using the navy in modern conditions of possible combat operations will greatly differ from those which have dominated in past wars, including the Second World War. Therefore, in considering the navy as the most important of the components of the sea power of the state, we shall deal, though briefly, with certain principles of the use of a modern fleet which the theory of naval art is now evolving.

A most important feature of the current stage in the development of naval art is the intensive extension of its size and composition and the increasingly many-sided elaboration of new forms and ways of using the forces of the fleet at different operational levels. This is due primarily to the influence of scientific and technical progress, resulting in sharp qualitative changes in modes of combat, which ultimately means profound qualitative transformations in the material-technical base of armed struggle at sea. The formation and verification in the course of combat training and the constant improvement of new forms of using the forces of the fleet, new modes of operations in a different situation are naturally connected with change in the many categories, forming in their entirety the content of naval art. These categories are most sensitive to the transformation of all factors influencing the development of naval art. Therefore, changes in these categories may be regarded as the first manifestation of an objective multi-faceted process of the development of naval art as a whole.

Change in many categories of naval art and the impact of objective factors is manifest at all its levels. For example, one may speak of the interaction of the forces and control them in their strategic, operational and tactical aspects. This applies in equal measure to such concepts as maneuver, strike, concentration, and many others. At the same time such concepts as battle, attack and others are characteristic only of tactics.

Without considering the whole variety of categories relating the field of naval art we shall dwell only on those which may be used as an example, as it seems to us, to trace the general tendencies of the development of this branch of naval science.

Scope of Conflict

Increase in the potential of the fleet for solving strategic tasks determines the growth of its role and importance in war. A modern navy possesses universality and mobility and is capable of concentrating strike power which may be used not only for fighting a sea foe but also in the sphere of operations of other branches of the armed forces. Thanks to this, the scope of the armed struggle at sea is increasing to global proportions.

In looking at this category from the strategic angle it is also necessary to note the constantly growing ability of nuclear fleets to achieve ever more decisive objectives in a modern war. This particularly applies to the operations of the forces of the fleet aimed at wrecking the military-economic potential of the enemy, which may have a direct impact on the course, and even on the outcome, of a war.

The individual operations conducted by a fleet are greater and greater in scope. The expansion of the potential of a fleet in solving the tasks of destroying ground objectives results in an extension of the front and an increase in depth of the influence exercised by naval strategic weapons systems. For example, the potential of this influence by the American submarine strategic nuclear *Polaris-Poseidon* system in the past ten years has more than doubled. Hoping to go over to the new *Trident* submarine nuclear missile system, on which the Western press writes so much, the Americans expect to double its influence as compared with the *Polaris-Poseidon* system. It is also planned to widen its front of influence. With the completion of the change-over of the American armed forces to an oceanic strategy, apparently operations against ground objectives will also assume global proportions. The further extension of the spatial sweep of operations against ground objectives is not only a present but also a future tendency of the development of the naval art of nuclear fleets. Probably it is also manifest in operations in the sphere of combating naval strategic nuclear weapons systems which may encompass almost the whole extent of the World Ocean and assume a global character.

In looking at such an element of the scope of operations as the composition of usable forces, it must be noted that the sharp expansion of the potential of the forces in offense and defense is more and more often being achieved not only and not so much in the traditional way—simple increase in the number of ships and other weapon carriers. Increasing prominence is being assumed by such a factor as the increased ability of each ship to solve diverse tasks, using more sophisticated weapons. In other words, the prevailing criterion in evaluating the actual potential of the groupings of forces is now becoming not the number of carriers but their quality, expressed in the aggregate strike power of the weapons concentrated on them and combat tactical resources. For example, after the end of the Second World War in 1945 the submarine forces of the US fleet were represented by 263 submarines. Now, according to the data of *Jane's* reference work for 1973–74, this fleet totals only 127 submarines, 41 of which are atomic-powered missile carriers, 61 multi-purpose atomic ships and 25 diesels, although their total power bears no comparison with the power of earlier submarines. Thanks to their power they are a most important part of the strategic resources of the fleet of that country.

Groupings of other branches of the armed forces may, on an ever-increasing scale, form part of the forces enlisted to take part in operations in the oceanic theaters. This determines the new possibilities for total realization of a further category of naval art, stemming from the strategy of armed conflict in the oceanic theaters of military operations-interactions. Its advent in the framework of a unified military strategy, in turn, is nothing other than an expression of the continuing process of shaping the categories of naval art corresponding to the modern material means of waging armed conflict.

STRIKE

The growth of the power of naval weapons at a particular stage of its development brought a quite new understanding of such a category as strike. Earlier the concept of strike was accompanied by the modifying adjectival definitions "gun," "torpedo," "bomb" and at one time "ram"; that is, this category was considered only a tactical concept and only in individual cases, for example in the expression "strike from the sea," did it assume the importance of a concept of operational status. Now the concept of strike has been extended to the attaining of strategic goals. It is considered that strike is becoming the dominant form of use of forces since it allows modern combat operations to realize their full potential from enormous distances and different directions, and thereby even attain such a strategic objective as devastation of the military-economic potential of an enemy.

In operational art, the strike is increasingly asserting itself as one of the basic methods of solving combat tasks. The strike in each operation is not only the totality of the specific combat actions welded together by unity of purpose or tasks. It may also be independent and even a single-act operation of a single weapons carrier or a group of them. For example, a strike on a grouping of surface forces may be delivered by a group of ships armed with guided missiles. Naval aviation is equally able to discharge such a task.

In the tactical link the strike, unlike in the past, when it was only one among elements of a battle and was regarded as a set of attacks, held together by the unity of a tactical task, is increasingly becoming tantamount to a battle. For example, by delivering a strike on a submarine of an enemy or the missiles launched by it, the combat task may be solved. A large surface ship may be destroyed by a strike by one submarine using long-range missiles. The further development of this tendency is promoted by the constant increase in the range and power of naval weapons, which makes it impossible in certain conditions to solve tactical tasks not by sustained and stubborn opposition but by a unilateral, single-act action against the enemy.

Thus, strategic, operational and tactical objectives can be reached by strikes. In individual cases the strike delivered "under the norms and rules of tactics," for example, by missiles from a submarine on land targets, can immediately bring strategic results. This is an already new quality in a category as customary for us as the strike, which is undergoing changes in the process of development of the material base of armed struggle at sea and its necessary naval art.

BATTLE

The battle always was and remains the main means of solving tactical tasks. For a long time it remained the sole form of combat use of the navy. Like any phenomenon, battle undergoes continuous evolution. One of the features of the process is an increase in the distances of combat clashes and their spatial sweep, determined by the growth of the range of action of naval weapons, maneuverability in different planes and media, independent operational potential and range of sailing (flight) of its carriers and also by participation in battle of other branches of the forces of the fleet, primarily aviation. At the dawn of the development of the fleets it was practically impossible to say anything about the distances over which battles were fought, since the solution of the task was determined by the possibilities of capturing an enemy by boarding or by ramming him. Gradually, the range of action of weapons increased and ships on opposing sides became capable of striking the enemy at ever greater distances. Already in the years of the Second World War they began to exceed not only the range of optical visibility but also the range of technical means of observation existing at the time.

The first battle at sea which paved the way for "non-contact" combat operations of ships was the engagement off Midway Island on 4 June 1942. In modern conditions these ranges already run into several hundreds of kilometers. And it may be confidently stated that in the future the sea battle will, as a rule, proceed over enormous spaces, and ascertaining the situation will be possible only with the aid of special essentially aerial or cosmic devices.

Development of the sea battle as a form of utilization of fleet forces has always been attended by change in its three-dimensional character. At first the battle represented a clash of the surface forces only on the surface of the water, then it embraced the underwater and aerial media. Ever-growing importance in a modern sea battle is being assumed by its specific attributes, expressed in the fact that the opposing sides are directing an ever greater part of their efforts at combating the torpedo or missile already released by the enemy, gradually cutting down the share of the effort aimed at destroying the carriers of these weapons. Thus, the sea battle is already assuming a new quality.

In many cases the battle may not include such an obligatory element of the past as tactical deployment. Deployment may be carried out in good time. In this case, to construct the most rational combat orders with changes in the tactical situation as a result of maneuver by a probable enemy or with a change in the composition of his forces, the forces may be pre-deployed. It is assumed that the elements of tactics forming the content of the classical scheme of the sea battle—seek out the enemy, tactical deployment and delivery of strikes after the weapon carrier has moved into the release position—will also persist in the future.

The strike and defensive potential of the forces of the fleet is constantly increasing and this gives grounds for asserting that in the future, to overcome the organized and deeply-staggered defense battle of the enemy in a battle, tactical interaction of diverse forces will be necessary. However, in individual cases, because of the sharp growth of the strike potential of the forces of the fleet, outstripping their defensive capacities, the waging of a battle with homogenous forces will apparently also remain realistic.

The further growth of the destructive power of weapons and timely deployment will shorten the time for solving combat tasks. The quickening of the pace of development of events will introduce changes in a category such as the battle. It will become more fleeting, dynamic and productive.

A special feature of the sea battle is that it has nearly always been waged to destroy the enemy. The equipping of the forces of the fleets with nuclear weapons is further accentuating this feature.

INTERACTION

Interaction is, as is known, one of the most important categories of naval art. The rational combination of offensive and defensive potential of diverse groupings, compensating the weak points of some forces by the strong points of others, helps to solve tasks considerably exceeding those which are solved by the usual coordination of homogenous forces.

The organization of interaction, as the range of weapons, their diversity, power and speed of their carriers increased, has steadily become more complicated. At present its importance and potential are growing, thanks to the development of the means of communication and control.

Under the influence of scientific and technical progress, technical means of combat are becoming more sophisticated and therefore new possibilities for mutual penetration into the spheres of combat actions of other branches of the armed forces are appearing. The importance of tactical and operational interaction in solving any task by the fleet is growing. Tactical interaction of non-homogenous forces in combating nuclear missile weapon-carriers will be organized where there is an acute need to solve the task in the shortest time possible.

The potential for other branches of the armed forces operating jointly with the fleet in the sphere of tasks of the latter, like the possibilities for the fleet solving tasks on land and in the air, will steadily increase.

The extension of the sphere of combat operations of branches of the armed forces will undoubtedly complicate the organization of their interaction at operational and strategic levels.

Thus, in the near future the organization of interaction will become even more complicated, the degree of its importance will grow and its forms and methods will become more varied.

MANEUVER

The maneuver is the oldest category of naval art. Fire and maneuver for long practically formed the core of naval tactics. Thanks to the maneuver, the forces of the fleet were able to bring weapons to such a level where the possibilities of these weapons could be fully realized in a strike, and, in addition, in certain cases the necessary concentration of forces be achieved. It should be noted that as the range of weapons lengthened, maneuver in battle carried out at tactical deployment stage constantly contracted linearly. With the appearance of naval guns, it was no longer necessary to draw up to the enemy and the maneuver became shorter. When naval ordnance became rifled, it contracted still further and after the advent of rockets, with a flight range beyond the horizon and high accuracy of hit of the target, assumed new qualities. The replacement in considerable measure of the maneuver of the weapon carrier by the maneuver with trajectories of weapons proved quite realistic. For example, the area within which it is possible to strike at the enemy with naval armaments with a firing range of 20km is 1256 sq. km. With use of missiles with a firing range of 200km, this area will be equal to 125,600 sq. km. If it is remembered that with increase in the firing range of weapons by one order of magnitude the area which can be hit by them by two orders of magnitude, then it is not difficult to imagine the scale of the potential of the maneuver with trajectories of rockets with a firing range of several thousands of kilometers. However, from this it does not follow that the importance of the maneuver of forces in a battle will decline, but it will be simpler to undertake.

On the other hand, the maneuver of forces beyond the limits of observation of the enemy who, in turn, takes measures to occupy an advantageous position, also beyond the limits of observation, requires it to be backed by reconnaissance and target indication data. The maneuver will be carried out on the basis of data received from different radio-electronic sources and in the conditions of the most intensive electronic countermeasures which, given correct organization, may completely paralyze the system of monitoring the situation and the receipt of information. Therefore the carrying out of the maneuver and use of different technical means for monitoring the situation and target designation demand true art. The acute need arises for coherent interaction of strike groups, not only with the reconnaissance forces but also with the units of external target designation. Undoubtedly, it will still be necessary to secure a maneuver and concentrate forces, equipped with such short range weapons as the torpedo and guns, which unquestionably will continue to remain for arming the fleets of the future.

Maneuver with ship forces in the future will become swifter with the wide introduction of ships with dynamic support principles into many fleets of the world.

In considering the maneuver from the operational angle, we would note that its importance as a form of operation aimed at ensuring the operational deployment of forces and concentrating them in particular areas of the oceanic theaters will greatly grow in the future.

SPEED

This is a characteristic of modern naval art particular to all forms and variants of combat operations at sea. Its expression is connected with the development of the means of armed struggle, thanks to which the former ways of waging a sea battle, made up of a sustained maneuver of the forces and their repeated and prolonged action on the enemy, have gradually lost their importance and have been replaced by dynamic, swift, decisive and increasingly productive combat clashes.

Scientific and technical progress is leading to the creation of ever more mobile weapon-carriers and long-range high-speed means of attack. In the future, therefore, speed will be an integral feature of any operation, battle or strike.

Its manifestation in the operational link will be expressed in further contraction of the duration of action on an enemy, with a simultaneous rise in the power and impact of strikes and combat operations, making up the content of sea operations.

It is precisely the speed of the different groupings of forces aimed at the most important enemy objectives which will become a decisive factor in choosing how they are used. Speed ensures the fullest use of all the combat potential of the forces for the quickest attainment of their objectives in operations and makes their strikes inescapable and irresistible.

The saturation of armed struggle at sea with swiftly-moving operations, strikes and other combat actions makes this struggle particularly dynamic and highly effective. Therefore the combat activity of fleets in the future will be a complex combination of simultaneous and successive swift, rapid combat actions culminating in the attainment of decisive goals and exerting in particular cases a direct influence on the course and outcome of the armed conflict as a whole.

The importance of speed—this most important factor in armed conflict at sea—will grow and the ability to carry out swift actions will become the most important indicators of the mastery of naval art.

TIME

With the development of naval technology, increase in the speeds of weapon carriers and the range and power of weapons, naval art was faced with the need to solve growing tasks more and more rapidly.

Already in the years of the Second World War the destruction of a particular grouping of the enemy was not always limited to a strictly defined time interval. If, for example, the task was to destroy an enemy convoy en route at sea, it could be solved at any moment during its passage, lasting days and even weeks. And whether the task set was accomplished at the start or end of this period was not of fundamental importance. The only important thing was to accomplish it while the grouping of enemy ships was at sea.

Now such an approach will often be inapplicable. In a number of cases the groupings of the forces of an enemy fleet will have to be destroyed in a definite very short time interval, before they can make full use of their weapons.

An important feature of the change in the significance of the category considered is that the time necessary for solving strategic tasks by the fleet after the start of military operations will be of the same order as the time necessary for solving tactical tasks.

As the means of armed conflict at sea continue to develop, this will become increasingly obvious. The growing demands for shortening the times of solving tasks decisive for the development of all forms of armed conflict at sea have made it necessary to keep the forces of the fleet in readiness for immediate delivery of strikes on the enemy and all-round automation of the control of these forces.

In considering the categories of naval art it is also desirable to take a look at the creation of certain conditions which ensure the attainment by the forces of the fleet of the goals set. Without going into the whole diversity of such conditions, we feel it necessary to dwell on those ensuring the freedom of action of their forces in a battle and operation, and, at the same time, creating serious interference for the enemy. In other words we have in mind what is often called dominance in the area of operations of one's forces or simply dominance at sea.

DOMINANCE AT SEA

There is a special category particular solely to the armed conflict in maritime theaters. The naval forces do not form a line of a front, they are mobile, their operations are not connected with moving through, capture or retention of certain spaces. They operate on 'no man's water' in stretches where there is no 'sovereign' ruler since international conventions recognize the principle of the sea open (free) to all. A victor in a sea battle or an operation does not always hurry to quit the battlefield as it is done, for example, by submarines after an attack, although it may have resulted in heavy enemy losses. However, any fleet always seeks to create in a particular area of the sea the regime necessary for it, for example, to gain control of shipping and ensuring its safety, freedom to deploy one's forces, etc.

Naval losses are hard to make good. Therefore, each defeat inflicted on an enemy means not only the achievement of the goal of the given combat clash but the creation of favorable conditions for quite a long time for solving the next task. It largely deprives the enemy of the possibility, sometimes for a long time, of undertaking organized action of an offensive nature and creates a very specific situation. This situation is characterized by the fact that the victor is free to choose the time, directions and character of the offensive operations, sometimes using for this even weak groupings of his forces.

Depriving the enemy of the possibility of staging a determined counter-action, the victor can exploit this victory by severing the sea shipments of the enemy by blockading his ports, bases and coastal areas, seizing islands and some distant territories or can deliver without hindrance strikes against the shore.

For the defeated side, if its economy was closely dependent on sea communications or if its fleet was the main part of its armed forces, loss of dominance at sea in the distant past could have meant even defeat in a war.

In speaking of the "age" of this category of naval art, then without fear of error it may be boldly asserted that history does not know of a more ancient and hardier concept. The idea of dominance at sea appeared when the use of the sea spaces began to be used in wars by specially created organized naval forces.

Close attention to dominance at sea was paid in the period of colonial seizures, carried out with the aid of the fleet of the powers of western Europe, primarily England, which, to justify her striving for world dominance by colonial robbery and piracy, used the flighty expression of the well-known English adventurer and pirate Walter Raleigh: "He who is master of the sea is master of world trade. And he who is master of world trade is master of the riches of the earth and of the earth itself." This ominous assertion was more than once repeated by Winston Churchill and now serves as the banner of bellicose circles of English and American imperialism.

The regular Russian navy, the creation of which is associated with the name of Peter the Great, by its resolute actions conveniently demonstrated an understanding of the essence of the idea of dominance at sea and the ability to put this idea into practice. Shattering the sea power of Sweden in the Baltic, it gained for itself freedom of action in the most important areas of the theater and skillfully used it to force the enemy to sign a peace treaty. The idea of dominance at sea was maintained and developed by the great Russian military chiefs—Suvorov, Potemkin, Ushakov, Spiridov and others.

On dominance at sea and its importance in the course of a war, Engels wrote in 1865: ". . . If one dominates at sea . . . this is an advantage."[4]

In the textbook on naval tactics written for the Russian naval corps in 1873, twenty years earlier than the work on this question appeared in England and the USA, Lieutenant Captain Berezin clearly outlined the theory of dominance at sea and ways of achieving it. There it was stated: "When a war begins, involving the fleets, attaining dominance at sea is usually the first and principal task. If the forces are greatly incommensurate this task is solved by direct blockade of the roads or the harbors where the hostile squadrons are, and then, of the whole shore; in absence of such incommensurability it is necessary to gain this dominance by inflicting defeats (squadron engagements) on the hostile fleet and only then establish a blockade seeking to destroy the sea trade of the enemy and all his

---

4. F. Engels, *Selected Military Works* (in Russian), pp. 666–67, Moscow, Voenizdat, 1956.

transport by sea." Further Berezin asserted that dominance cannot be absolute, that as well as blockade it is necessary to send cruisers in pursuit of separate vessels of the enemy, that inshore landing operations are possible even without dominance at sea, etc.

Unlike the interpretation of the idea of dominance at sea adopted in Russia, in England, the biggest colonial power in the world, where the "exploitation of the colonies was the principal source of enrichment of the British bourgeoisie and maintenance of colonial dominance constituted its principal military task,"[5] political meaning was vested in this concept. In this connection the maintenance and dominance at sea became for the English capital a matter of survival. The idea became the basic guiding principle of English military doctrine.

The idea of dominance at sea was taken as the basis of English military doctrine by Admiral Colomb and his followers. The USA, hurrying by the beginning of the epoch of imperialism, to occupy a leading place among the claimants to world dominance, developed its own theories of dominance at sea, the progenitor of which is recognized to be Admiral Mahan.

Both these authors in the expositions fulfilled the social mission of nascent imperialism and therefore transformed the category of naval art into a political concept of the bourgeoisie bent on world dominance, into an ideological banner of imperialism. The gaining of dominance at sea was proclaimed as the sole aim of armed struggle at sea, the attainment of which ensures, in their view, the establishment of world dominance.

It is known that serious attention was paid to dominance at sea as a category of naval art by Lenin, making a profound scientific analysis of the causes of the defeat of Russia in the 1904–05 Russo-Japanese war. He wrote: "The Japanese have so far more rapidly and heavily reinforced their military forces after each major engagement than the Russians. And now having won complete dominance at sea and the total destruction of one of the Russian armies they will be able to send twice as many reinforcements as the Russians."[6]

Subsequently, the category of dominance at sea was studied and elaborated in the Soviet navy. Thus, in the 1930 Combat Regulations for the

---

5. M.V. Frunze, *Selected Works* (in Russian), Vol. II, p. 12, Moscow, Voenizdat, 1957.

6. V.I. Lenin, *Complete Collected Works* (in Russian), Vol. 9, p. 154.

naval forces it was emphasized that it is necessary to create such conditions as will guarantee the secure movement of forces at sea from their bases and the solution by them of the combat task. These conditions include: countering a blockade of the enemy, both by correct choice of the support points, making it difficult for him to continue the blockade, and by combat operations proper to make a blockade impossible or lessen its effectiveness, countering enemy reconnaissance and patrol service.

It must be noted that from the very inception Soviet naval science has completely rejected attempts to equate the concept of 'dominance at sea' with the concept of 'dominance over the world.' It always saw the gaining of dominance at sea not as an end in itself but merely a way of creating certain conditions enabling the forces and resources of the fleet to solve successfully particular tasks in specific areas of the theater in a defined period of time. Therefore, in the Soviet fleet in pre-war years, the term 'favorable operational regime' was more widely adopted. In our Regulations it was stressed that this term means the conditions promoting successful solution of the tasks set before the fleet. By these conditions were meant those elements of the situation which make it possible to form the necessary groupings of the forces of the fleet, deliver strikes and perform the combat tasks set without seriously departing from the scheduled plan. To create these conditions it was necessary to wage a stubborn and sometimes quite long struggle with the use of different forces and resources at sea, in the air and in a number of cases in the coastal areas.

In the course of the Great Patriotic War in the basic documents regulating the combat activity of the fleet, the actions of its forces to create the necessary situation for its operations were classified as actions creating the most favorable and stable operational regime in the stationing areas and on the most important communications. Analysis of the combat experience of our fleets helps to define more clearly a number of definitions relating to this category of naval art. At the end of the 'forties, dominance at sea was regarded as the creation of conditions promoting the successful conduct by the fleets of operations at sea and by the sea fronts on land. Strategic dominance at sea (in a theater) was recognized as the best of these conditions. It was characterized by a favorable position (ratio of forces, their stationing, equipment of theater, etc.) when the enemy in the whole theater was not in a position to disrupt operations undertaken by us. In passing we would note that the concept of the sea theater of combat operations then only referred to the seas directly adjoining the territory of the Soviet Union.

If strategic dominance in a sea theater was absent, and this was very typical of that time, then the necessary condition for the successful conduct of sea operations was recognized by the gaining of tactical dominance. By such dominance was understood superiority in forces and resources in the direction of the main strike, achieved by wide and bold maneuver with the forces, both in the preparatory stage of the operation and in the course of it, and skillful utilization of the geographic features of the sea theater and of its equipment.

The difference between strategic and tactical dominance, in the views at that time, consisted only in the size of the space controlled and the duration of the time interval in the course of which this dominance could be held. If strategic dominance served the ends of waging war or a campaign, then tactical dominance served the ends of conducting an operation, a series of battles or even one battle.

The inner content of these two concepts—favorable tactical situation gained for conducting an operation or battle in a particular area of a sea theater in a period necessary for the reliable warranty of success and a guarantee against the disruption by the enemy preparation and waging of an operation or battle—remained the same.

With the advent of nuclear weapons, and then missiles, many theoreticians claimed that the question of gaining dominance at sea had receded into the background because new combat and technical means of armed conflict at sea had radically altered the conditions of conducting operations and combat activities, and hence the means of maintaining them.

One of the arguments for denying the need to gain dominance at sea was the claim that since combat activities had become swift and productive, the forces waging a struggle at sea did not need the creation of favorable conditions. Often the question was even posed thus: "What will a fleet do in a nuclear war—destroy the enemy or gain dominance, running the risk of being destroyed by the enemy before he can reach his goals?"

As shown by history, with the development of the material-technical base of the fleets and increase in their combat potential new features of the struggle for dominance at sea came into being, although this struggle itself remained a reflection of the objective reality, determined by the specifics of combat actions at sea.

The growth of the speed of ships and other forces of the fleet and the improvement of the means of communication and reconnaissance have considerably shortened the time span during which dominance at sea can be held. Thus, the English sailing fleet after the battle of Aboukir (1798) established its dominance of the Mediterranean for some years, which accounted for the failure of the Napoleonic expedition to Egypt, despite the fact that French troops had already been landed and had won a series of major victories in land engagements. Dominance of the Japanese fleet gained at the end of 1941 as a result of the smashing of the battle forces of the US Navy in Pearl Harbor and sinking of English battleships in the Gulf of Siam lasted no more than four months.

From these examples it will be seen that the period of keeping the dominance gained at sea tends to shorten and the struggle for gaining it becomes even tougher. This tendency still persists, since the forces and resources of the fleets are being vigorously developed, nuclear missile weapons perfected and naval aviation is coming into ever wider use. It is particularly important to note that submarines have become the main branch of the forces of modern fleets. A major role is also played by the new strategic orientation of the fleets for struggle against the shore. All this is making more necessary the all-round backing of the actions of the forces solving strategic tasks. Therefore, the struggle to create, in a particular area of a theater and in a particular time, favorable conditions for successfully solving by a large grouping of forces of the fleet, the main tasks facing it, and at the same time creating conditions such as would make it more difficult for the enemy to fulfill his tasks and prevent him from frustrating the actions of the opposing side, will apparently be widely adopted.

The creation of the conditions for gaining dominance at sea has always taken a long time and demanded a number of measures even in peacetime. Among these measures are the creation and preparation of the necessary forces and resources for keeping them in readiness to solve combat tasks, from groupings of forces and such deployment of them in a theater as to ensure positional superiority over the enemy, and also equipping of the sea and oceanic theaters of military operations, the corresponding organization of the forces and system of emplacement, the system of control of them, etc., and which serve their purpose.

The interrelationship and interdependence of combat actions of the fleet in solving the main tasks in gaining dominance at sea consist and will evidently continue to consist in the fact that the areas and directions in which dominance at sea is achieved and the time it is held, completely depend on the conditions of fulfillment of the main tasks. Combat actions, the aim of which is to ensure dominance at sea in selected areas or in particular directions, may either precede the solution by the fleet of the main tasks or be conducted simultaneously. Consequently, the attainment of dominance at sea is a factor ensuring the success of the actions of the forces solving the main tasks. The successful solution by the fleet of these main tasks ensures the further securing of it of dominance at sea and widening of the sphere of its implementation.

The experience of the Great Patriotic War showed that the success of the actions of land forces and the capture by them of new coastal areas also help to gain dominance at sea. An example of this is the gaining and securing of dominance of our fleets in the Black, Baltic and Barents Seas as a result of the operations conducted by land forces together with the fleets. The German command strove for dominance in the Black and Baltic Seas by capturing the bases of the Soviet fleet from the land. However, the Hitlerites failed to reach this goal. Their plans were foiled by the joint actions of the Soviet army and navy. From this it may be concluded that the gaining of dominance at sea depends both on the solution of the main tasks set before the fleet and on the general course of the armed struggle as a whole.

One cannot help noticing that in undertaking military preparations the imperialists are seeking to create the conditions for gaining dominance at sea at the very start of a war. The idea is to widen the sphere of dominance at sea to the depths of the oceans and the air space above them.

From all this it follows that such a category of naval arts as the gaining of dominance at sea retains its topicality and therefore the elaboration of it in all its aspects relevant to the present, forms one of the important tasks of naval science.

Consequently, the general perspectives of the development of naval art are connected with the continuous growth of demands for the most effective use of the means of combat, the stiffening of the norms of training and use of weapons, rise in the intensity of combat actions, shortening of the times of decision-making and increase in the responsibility of the flag officer. The appearance of long-range and homing weapons, highly effective cybernetic and automated systems is increasing still further the role of humans in armed conflict at sea.

Important tendencies in the development of naval art are the progressive widening of the object of its investigation, the fields of optimization, and an increase in the role of engineering-technical and physic-mathematical sciences definitely required for solving the theoretical questions of naval art.

Awaiting elucidation are the perspectives of development of such elements of naval art as reconnaissance, camouflage, operational and tactical deployment, combat orders, defense, rear back-up and others.

CHAPTER FIVE

Navies, Power, and Prosperity

When the "Gorshkov articles" were published in the early 1970s, first in *Morskoy Sbornik* and then in translation in *Proceedings*, they were pored over by Western analysts. It is difficult in today's twenty-four-hour media, multi-source, information-age world to comprehend the significance that they were afforded. By then Gorshkov had been at the helm of the Red Navy for almost twenty years and his views *were* news, at least to those in the small world of Cold War naval policy. Western analysts debated whether Gorshkov's writings were authorized or whether they were an attempt to influence the direction of policy inside the Soviet military hierarchy, and about what they *really* meant. Every word and phrase was considered for inference and some analysts claimed to find significant meaning in semi-hidden nuances of language.

The whole series is not repeated here, but a compendium of Gorshkov's work would be incomplete without some acknowledgment of the place of these articles in naval history. This chapter and the next bookend that era with the first and last of the eleven articles reproduced as they appeared in *Proceedings* in 1974. It is not known precisely when the articles were written (they were first published in Russian in 1972 and so were probably written in 1971), but it is noteworthy that their English version was being widely read in the immediate aftermath of the Arab-Israeli Yom Kippur War, a war that was accompanied by U.S.-Soviet naval brinkmanship in the Mediterranean. They were topical and became required reading for the professional officer of the day. It was also the year that Admiral Zumwalt, the U.S. chief of naval operations, stated in an interview with the *New York Times* his conviction that the United States had lost control of the sea-lanes to the Soviet Union.

Rather than reinterpret them completely, the two "Navies in War and Peace" articles below are treated at face value, albeit with a twenty-first-century eye. They are substantial in their own right, eloquently written (probably more so than any of the earlier or later stand-alone *Morskoy Sbornik* pieces—suggesting that they had been refined for external consumption), and they tell their own story of sea power from the perspective of a continental actor trying to break the Western stranglehold on maritime superiority.

The first is a scene setter that reaffirms the age-old role of navies as instruments of foreign policy. That thesis was not new then and is certainly not new now, but Gorshkov gave it an interesting slant. Today's reader might expect a mid-twentieth-century communist to equate sea power with international political relations, but he was also acutely aware of the direct and positive relationship between navies, national power, and economic prosperity. He gave a potted history of the world through a maritime lens, moving from antiquity through feudalism to capitalism in just a few pages, and he succinctly associated the achievement and, crucially, the maintenance of "great power" status with naval might—navies enabling, supporting, and protecting trading nations. He was, presumably, projecting his narrative toward what he believed would come next: world communism or, at least, a post-capitalist world.

To the familiar theme of sea power leading to economic power, Gorshkov added an additional factor rarely found in contemporary writing. He focused on the influence of social systems on the development of armed forces. In essence, in his first article in the "Navies in War and Peace" series Gorshkov described a virtuous cycle in which societal change drove military change, which led to increased international power and thence to prosperity, which, in turn, became the engine of further societal change.

In today's world, fixated as it is on globalization and the interconnectedness of the "system," navalists would tend to agree with much of Gorshkov's basic premise. However, Gorshkov also cautioned against overreliance on maritime power as a policy instrument and its potential to atrophy if governments simply assumed that their global ranking was assured in perpetuity. In words that with hindsight could equally be applied to the downfall of the Soviet Union, Gorshkov cited sixteenth-century Spain's descent to "third-rate" status, despite her "unbeatable armada," as a consequence of political backwardness and an inability to innovate. Political agility is always important. A more successful role model of the past, he mused, might be Great Britain. British "perfidiousness" and her ability to largely limit participation in wars to the sea, leaving any requirement to fight on land in the hands of continental powers, kept her at the top table—and kept her rich. (Though he also emphasized his assessment that despite the importance of the Battle of Trafalgar the real architects of Napoleon's downfall at the beginning of the eighteenth century were, in fact, Russian.)

Twenty-first-century actors, playing on the stage of post-industrial, post-modern, and, perhaps, edging toward post-military societies, might consider Gorshkov's views on sea power and, in particular, the role of navies to be dated. He did concentrate much of his attention on the war-fighting role of navies, but he did not limit his discourse there. Often framing his argument in geographical terms and pointing to the physical extent of the maritime environment, he saw no false divide between the actions and activity of one arm of society (the state's navy—the source of security) and others (fishing fleets and industrial complexes—the sources of food, raw materials, and energy). Of course, it was easier for a communist with an uncompromising belief in state-planned economies to make that case, but it is not dissimilar in its core argument and outcomes to the U.S. Navy's cooperative strategy for twenty-first-century sea power.

Whatever size, shape, and configuration navies and other sea services adopt now and in the future, the relationship between them and the type of societies that they stem from will be apparent. They will be relied on to be prepared to fight their nation's or their society's wars, but they will also be expected to protect and help shape the "system" that their masters see as best to further their interests.

NAVIES IN WAR AND PEACE

U.S. Naval Institute *Proceedings*, 1974

For many centuries the ocean expanses have not only been a convenient means of communication between continents and between the suppliers of products vitally essential to mankind, but also an arena of fierce struggle and military conflicts. The scale of utilizing the water medium for military aims, i.e., for the defense of one's own country and to seize overseas possessions, has grown in relation to man's knowledge and mastery of the ocean. At the present time, in an era of far-reaching scientific discoveries and the utilization of them for military needs, the capabilities for conducting combat operations on the oceanic expanses have increased incredibly, while the naval arms race abroad, and the creation of diverse means of naval combat have reached unprecedentedly imposing scales.

The hallmark of naval forces is their high degree of maneuverability, and ability to concentrate secretly and to form powerful groupings which are of surprise to the enemy. At the same time, naval forces are more stable against the effects of nuclear weaponry than land forces. All of this has catapulted the navies into the front ranks of the diverse, modern means of armed combat. Their employment in nuclear-missile warfare is related to the introduction of much of what is new in tactics and operational skills, in ship design, and in the outfitting of ships with equipment and armament.

The qualitative transformations which have taken place in naval forces have also changed the approach to evaluating the relative might of navies and their combat groupings. We have had to cease comparing the number

Sergei Georgiyevich Gorshkov, "Navies in War and Peace," U.S. Naval Institute *Proceedings* 100, no. 1 (January 1974), pp. 18–27.

of warships of one type or another and their total displacement (or the number of guns in a salvo, or the weight of this salvo), and turn to a more complex, but also more correct appraisal of the striking and defensive power of ships, based on a mathematical analysis of their capabilities and qualitative characteristics.

The military technical revolution is constantly introducing new things in all areas of military affairs, but the final goals of naval warfare remain the same: the defeat of the enemy and the destruction of his vital forces and materiel (i.e., his ships with their crews and weapons stores, and weapons or shore objectives located within range). Therefore, combat operations at sea, just as on land, by obeying the general laws of the dialectic which are constantly in effect, cannot be conducted separately from the goals of that policy which led to the war. Therefore, in today's context it is interesting to trace, from a historical standpoint, the dialectical relationship between the development of naval forces and the state policy goals which they were intended to serve.

V. I. Lenin pointed out that "Every war is inseparably linked with the political system from which it stems. That very policy which a certain power and a certain class within this power conducted for a long time prior to a war, inevitably and unavoidably will be continued by this same class during a war, changing only the form of action." And further, "Policy is reason, while war is only the instrument, and not the opposite. Consequently, it only remains to subordinate the military point of view to the political."[1]

The basic and sole means of waging armed conflict between states has always been the army and navy, which in peacetime have continued to serve as the instrument or weapon of state policies. Many examples from history attest to the fact that in the age of feudalism and capitalism all problems of foreign policy were always decided on the basis of, and taking into account, the military power of the "negotiating" sides, and that the potential military might of one state or another, built up in accordance with its economic capabilities and political orientation, permitted it to conduct a policy advantageous to itself to the detriment of other states not possessing corresponding military power.

---

1. Leninskiy sbornik (Collection of Lenin's Articles) XII, 2nd ed., 1931, p. 437.

The development of armed forces is linked in the most direct manner to the history of social-economic systems, and to the methods of material production characteristic of them. The flourishing or decline of them is determined by the process of the formation or decay of one social system or another. Thus, these periods when one social-economic system was being replaced by another, more progressive system have given considerable impetus to progress in the military area.

Technical discoveries have always had a revolutionizing effect on the development of armed forces and on the art of employing them. This demonstrates the pattern of the influence on the military field of the society's economic development and the growth of its productive forces. In this connection, V. I. Lenin wrote: "Military tactics depend on the level of development of military equipment . . ."[2]

Such highly important factors as the social and political system, the social composition of the people from whom the armed forces are drawn, the extent of combat training, the level of knowledge, and the moral make-up of the personnel also affect the condition of the armed forces and the level of the art of their employment. In turn, the above qualities depend on the character of the leaders of the fighting men.

Marxism considers the geographic environment, which also influences the character and direction of the development of armed forces, to be one of the constant and invariable conditions in the development of human society. Among the many elements embraced by the concept of the geographical environment and affecting the development of mankind, and, consequently, also of the armed forces of states, are the seas and oceans. In solving problems of commerce, of reliable routes of communication, of relationships between peoples, and of the fishing and maritime industries, men back in ancient history had already opened up individual littoral areas of the seas and oceans. The maritime location of many countries fostered the development in them of specific areas of industry (e.g., shipbuilding, the catching and processing of fish and marine animals, etc.) which had a beneficial effect on the overall progress of these countries that, naturally, also left an impression on the development of the armed forces of the states which, to one degree or another, were engaged in the

---

2. V. I. Lenin. Poln. sobr. soch. (Complete Collected Works), Vol. 13, p. 374.

construction of navies and to a greater or lesser degree employed them in wars.

In different historical eras the above factors have had a definite effect on the character and structure of the armed forces which were made up of various components. Without resorting to a detailed examination of the changes in the structure of the armed forces of states on a historical plane, let us simply note that all maritime countries, without exception, usually have had (or strove to have) both ground forces and a navy. Apropos of this, Peter I said: "Every potentate who has only ground forces has only one hand; yet whoever has a navy too, has both hands." The role and importance of each of them, at the level of development of technology and the economic capabilities which existed, were always determined by the unfolding political strategic situation and the mutual positions of the states or nature of the coalitions. In some stages of the history of states, ground forces have played the main role, and in others, the navy.

The place and role of each of the branches of a country's armed forces can change both in peacetime and in war depending on technical reorganization, on the enemy being confronted, the geographical conditions, etc. History presents many examples of this. From them we may recall the growth of the role of the Navy in the Northern War of 1700–1721, when Russia transferred operations from her own territory to the territory of the enemy, thereby forcing him to sign a peace treaty. Sometimes, however, wars which began with the Navy being predominantly important were ended by the overwhelming actions of the Army (for example, the Russo-Japanese War of 1904–1905). Clearly, in all cases, one aspect remains unchanged: the results of the victory in a campaign or war can only he secured by ground forces capable of confirming the reality of it by their actual presence.

Moreover, the experience of history attests to the fact that each branch of the armed forces makes its own certain and always discernible contribution to victory. To achieve victory, the presence of all branches of armed forces, properly organized, equipped, and trained, is essential. Each of them has its own specific features, sphere of employment, and conditions for concerted action. The skillful (or on the other hand, the unskillful) employment and the consideration of these specific features often determine the success (or failure) of operations, campaigns, or even the war as a whole.

In the modern context, in speaking of the military might of states, it is a matter of harmoniously combining all branches of developed and rationally balanced armed forces, and it is precisely because of this that the principle of cooperation among all branches of the armed forces is the basis of Soviet military doctrine. Only by coordinating their efforts can victory be achieved.

As early as 1921, M. V. Frunze wrote about this in works devoted to the building up of the Red Army. The idea of the decisive importance of coordinated actions by the Army and Navy in all areas of armed combat was vividly expressed in his work "A Single Military Doctrine and the Red Army."

An analysis of the employment of various branches of armed forces in time of war, or in peacetime, is of definite interest from the point of view of both the development of the art of war and the knowledge by the command personnel, of the specific features with which each of the branches of the armed forces is imbued.

Taking into account that such an understanding fosters the development of a unity of operational views in the command personnel of the armed forces, and is an indispensable and most important condition for skill in acting in concert, let us examine those questions applicable to the Navy, both in the historical and problem aspects. In this connection, we do not intend to cover the history of the naval art, much less define the prospects for the development of naval forces. We intend only to express a few thoughts about the role and place of navies in various historical eras, and at different stages in the development of military equipment, and of the art of war, in order, on this basis, to determine the trends and principles of the change in the role and position of navies in wars, and also in their employment in peacetime as an instrument of state policy. In this connection, the focus of attention on the Navy does not in any way imply any sort of unique importance of naval forces in modern armed combat, but stems from the above mentioned considerations.

Proceeding from the special features of the Navy as a military factor which can be used also in peacetime for purposes of demonstrating the economic and military power of states beyond their borders, and from the fact that over a period of many centuries it has been the solitary branch of armed forces capable of protecting the interests of a country beyond its borders, in our view it is useful to examine questions related to this specific feature of naval forces as a real component part of the military organization of a state.

In examining these questions, one should also take into account the ever growing interest in oceanic problems of various social quarters from different aspects—economic, political, and military—and in their dialectical relationship. In tracing the direct dependence of mankind on the World Ocean over the entire course of its centuries of history, it is impossible not to note how the ability of peoples to learn to appreciate the ocean, and to use it for their own needs, directly affects the growth of the political prestige of the country and its economic and military power.

Times Distant, Yet Important for Understanding: The Role of Navies

Navies have always played a great role in strengthening the independence of states whose territories are washed by seas and oceans, since they were an important instrument of policy. Naval might has been one of the factors which has enabled individual states to advance into the ranks of the great powers. Moreover, history shows that those states which do not have naval forces at their disposal have not been able to hold the status of a great power for very long.

And, it cannot be otherwise, for the sphere of naval operations are the seas and oceans which occupy seven-tenths of the surface of our planet. The continents are essentially gigantic islands whose total area is barely 150,000,000 square kilometers. They are surrounded, connected with one another, and kept in many respects (in particular, with regard to climate) in a constant state of dependence on the World Ocean, whose surface is equal to 350,000,000 square kilometers.

The seas and oceans serve as an inexhaustible source of diverse food resources, industrial raw materials, and energy. The most important and most economically advantageous routes of communications between countries, through which trade and other ties between peoples are carried out, pass through the seas and oceans. All of this determines the special role of the seas and oceans in the economy of states.

The development of maritime states has turned out to be so closely connected with the sea that, as a rule, their capitals and largest cities have grown up on the coasts. Seven of today's ten largest cities of the world are located on the shores of seas and oceans. The building-up, in the maritime countries, of many areas of industry and the economy dependent on the sea, which has brought about higher industrial development in these countries, has fostered the overall growth of the economy of maritime countries and the rate of growth. Therefore, it is not by accident that civilization, as a rule, originated and developed most often on the shores of seas and oceans. It is also not accidental that countries whose populations have been connected with seafaring have become economically strong earlier than others. Among these we may cite in various periods in history, Spain, England, Holland, France, Portugal, Turkey, and the U.S.A. All of the modern great powers are maritime states.

At the same time, for a long time wars have been waged not only on land, but also on the watery expanses, at first on rivers and lakes and in coastal areas of the seas, and later on the seas and oceans. Military necessity, the development of an economy related to the sea, and political conflict have always, and on an ever increasing scale, forced states to build, possess, and maintain naval forces on a modern level within the overall system of armed forces. At a certain stage of development, many states (primarily Holland, Spain, England, France, Japan, and the U.S.A.) have formulated their military strategy primarily on the basis of sea power.

Every social-economic system has built up armed forces, including navies, corresponding to its economic and technical capabilities. Thus, in the slave-holding society, galleys were the basis of the navies. In the era of feudalism, sailing ships appeared, which were developed more fully up to the moment of capitalism's entry into the world arena.

The scientific technical revolution of that day led, in the mid-19th century, to the following fundamental change in the material resources and equipment of naval forces—to the creation of the steam fleet, and later to undersea forces. And finally, recently even more profound and revolutionary changes have taken place in connection with the construction of the nuclear-powered navy of the nuclear-missile era.

These stages of naval development were not just stages in the technical improvement of warships. At the same time as the material resources and equipment were being altered, changes were also taking place in its position within the system of armed forces, in its basic mission, and in its role in the policy of the state in peacetime and in military operations at sea.

Even in ancient times, in solving problems concerning trade, routes of communications, ties between people, and of the fishing and marine industries, mankind developed several coastal areas of the seas and oceans. Parallel to this, knowledge was accumulated and expanded, at first about the individual regions of the earth; and later about the entire planet, including the World Ocean. It is difficult to overestimate the role of the Navy in this.

At the same time, from the era of the slave-holding society even up to our day, navies have been employed in numerous wars as the most important (and often the only) means of supporting the transport of military cargoes and land forces or the invasion by troops of the enemy territory, as well as to protect their own sea routes and to attack the enemy's merchant ships.

In the 16th to 17th centuries, one of the most important periods in the history of mankind began—the era of great geographical discoveries, the era of the initial accumulation of capital, and the development of capitalism. The major countries of Western Europe converted their navies into one of the instruments of the initial accumulation of capital: they were used to seize colonies, for the enslavement of peoples of entire continents, and to plunder them, and as the agents for the fierce struggles between rivals in the plundering of colonies, and also for control in the colonies and of the sea routes.

"The discovery of gold and silver mines in America, the eradication, enslavement, and the burning alive of the natives in pits, the first steps toward conquering and plundering East India, and the transformation of Africa into a preserve for hunting blacks—this was the dawning of the capitalist era of production."[3]

Spain and Portugal were the first to rush to discover new lands and colonize them. Sailing expeditions by Columbus, Magellan, Vasco da Gama, and other seafarers not only opened the American continent, extended the water route around Africa to India and China, and discovered many Pacific Ocean islands, but also initiated the colonization of these regions and countries. The English, French, and Dutch joined the Spanish and Portuguese in participating in the geographical discoveries and in the colonization of the new lands.

In the 16th century it seemed that Spain had firmly established a position as a great power, possessing vast colonies. But due to political backwardness

---

3. K. Marx, *Kapital*, Vol. 1, 1949, p. 754.

and the inability to compete with rapidly developing England, she was not able to exploit the riches plundered from the colonies, to rapidly develop her economy and her industry, and consequently, to build up armed forces, and particularly a navy, which were modern for that day. Soon after the defeat of the "unbeatable armada" by the more modern English Fleet, Spain, being in no condition to protect her overseas possessions, lost them and was gradually transformed from a great power into a third-rate state.

In the middle of the 17th century, Holland, which had taken the capitalist path of development earlier than the others, and had the strongest navy in the world at its disposal, became the largest colonial power and reached the apex of its power. But soon England, where industrial capital played the leading role as opposed to trade capital which held sway in Holland, became its main rival. The struggle between these countries became the hottest in several wars which history has named the Anglo-Dutch wars. The North Sea was the main arena for their struggles. After losing several naval battles and after attacks by the English from land, Holland acknowledged defeat and became a second-rate colonial power. Its fate was sealed by the victory of the industrial capital of England over Holland's trade capital, which was manifested militarily in the superiority of the English Fleet (or, in the final analysis, in the naval might of England).

Karl Marx wrote about this in this manner: ". . . Trade domination is now already related to the greater or lesser predominance of the conditions of the existence of major industry. It pays to compare, for example, England and Holland. The history of the fall of Holland as the dominant trade nation is a history of the subordination of trade capital to industrial capital."[4]

England also often used her Navy for direct enrichment. It is sufficient to recall that many English ships and merchantmen in the service of the King acted as pirates: they robbed the merchant ships of other countries, seized them, and dragged them away into English ports. Thus, instead of a consumer, the Navy became a source of enrichment to the state.

At the beginning of the 18th century, France also took the path of capitalist development. Through the enslavement of overseas countries, in

---

4. K. Marx. op. cit., Vol. 3, 1954, p. 345.

which the Navy played an important role, she was also transformed into a vast colonial empire possessing Canada, large territories in the Mississippi Valley, several West Indian islands, part of India, and broad regions in Africa. The core of England's policy was to attain the position of "Mistress of the Seas," personifying a world economic and political power; she chose to use every possible way to bring down her rivals at sea to the level of the states which were incapable of opposing her Navy as one way of achieving this goal. At this time the struggle in the world arena for economic hegemony, colonial possessions, and domination in world trade shifted to the sphere of rivalry between England and France. The culmination of this struggle was the so-called Seven Years War, in which almost all of the states of Europe were involved. "England and France fought over colonies in the Seven Years War, i.e., they waged an imperialistic war . . ."[5]

The principal events at that time unfolded at sea, as a result of which the navies played the most important role. The outcome of the battles between the English and French Fleets played a decisive role in achieving the political goals of this war. As a result of their hostilities, France, having lost any hope of domination, or even a predominant position on the sea and having lost control over the sea lanes, was forced to relinquish North America and India to England.

In the middle of the 18th century, having surpassed the other countries in economic development and possessing a developed industry and numerous colonies, England became the first world power. Backed by a powerful economy which provided England the supremacy of having the strongest fleet on the World Ocean, she assumed the leading position among the capitalist countries and held it for almost two centuries.

The desire of the British capitalists to hinder the development of industries in the colonies by every means, in order to keep them as mere suppliers of raw materials and as consumers of the goods of British industry, produced the war for independence of the more developed of its North American colonies. The navies of England's former rivals, France, Holland, and Spain acted on the colonies' behalf. The position of Russia, which declared a so called "armed neutrality," supported by the power of the Russian Navy, did not permit England to blockade America, also

---

5. V. I. Lenin, op. cit., Vol. 30, p. 7.

played a positive role for the Americans. The "mistress of the seas" had to fight a war under conditions in which her Navy was considerably inferior to the united fleet of the enemies. After England had lost several battles on land, considering the unfavorable relative strength of the forces on the sea which prevented unhindered supplying of reinforcements via the ocean, she was forced to recognize the independence of the United States of North America.

Despite the fact that the main missions in the war for independence were executed by the armies, it once more affirmed the growing influence of naval forces on the course and outcome of armed conflicts fought on land. In this war, naval operations were shifted from European waters to distant ocean regions which sharply increased the importance of communications, and problems of defending and hindering them in support of military actions on land arose on such a scale for the first time.

The new conditions of naval combat operations imposed higher demands on the seakeeping ability of the warships and on their combat stability. In connection with this, their dimensions were increased, designs were changed, armament strengthened, and subsequently armor made its appearance. The considerable growth in the capabilities of the rapidly developing capitalist industry fostered the building up of warship inventory, taking the new demands into account. All of this speeded up naval development, and at the turn of the 19th century permitted the naval role in political struggles and in military operations to be enhanced even further.

The main organizing force of the wars in the above period was the English bourgeoisie, which intended to seize France's remaining colonial possessions. In this connection, England tried to transfer the weight of the battles on the continent to her European allies, while limiting her participation in the wars mainly to operations at sea and against France's maritime territories.

It should be noted that the large bourgeoisie which came to power in France after the Thermidorian coup, also made it a primary task to reduce England's colonial power. Bonaparte's expedition into Egypt was undertaken for this purpose and with the future goal of seizing India. The French troops, which were transported across the sea unbeknownst to the English, began successful combat operations in Egypt. Within just two and a half months the English Fleet, under the command of Nelson, found the French warships anchored in Aboukir Bay and defeated them. The destruction of the French Fleet primarily affected the combat capability of that part of the army which was in Egypt and which turned out to be cut off from its main supply bases located in Europe. Moreover, it also affected the operations of the main forces of the French Army which, within six months of the defeat of the French Fleet at Aboukir, surrendered to the enemy, in a few months that which Bonaparte had won in his day in dozens of victorious battles.[6]

Thus, the weakness of the French Fleet became one of the main reasons for the failure of the plans for the conquest of Egypt, the passage to India, and the curtailing of English colonial power, even though France had the necessary ground forces at its disposal.

Continuing the struggle, Napoleon decided to land a large landing force directly on the British Islands, for which 2,343 diverse transport ships were readied. It seemed that a fatal threat hung over England. However, the preparation for the invasion was delayed. An attack, initiated by Russian troops under the command of Kutuzov, forced Napoleon to abandon entirely the landing of a force in England.

On 21 October 1805 in the Atlantic Ocean off the coast of Spain, the battle of Trafalgar took place in which the English, under the command of Nelson, inflicted a decisive defeat on the Franco-Spanish Fleet. The significance of this battle, as well as the role of the English Fleet in the struggle with Napoleonic France, were actually great, but were exaggerated to an even greater degree by a Western European historiographer who asserted that "at Trafalgar not only the greatest naval victory was won, but also the greatest and most remarkable victory of all those won on land and at sea in the course of the entire revolutionary war. No single victory nor any series of victories by Napoleon had such an effect on Europe."[7]

One cannot agree with this. As is well known, the struggle against Napoleon lasted many years and the main and decisive role in it was played by Russia, which destroyed the French Army in the Patriotic War of 1812. The victory gained by Russia actually had a greater effect on the political situation in Europe.

---

6. Ye. V. Tarle. *Napoleon*, Izd-vo AN SSSR, 1957, p. 74.

7. Fyffe's *History of Modern Europe*, Vol. 1, p. 281.

As for the Battle of Trafalgar, with respect to its consequences, it, of course, was not an ordinary military clash of fleets. After the series of defeats of the French Fleet, its final rout in this battle demonstrated France's inability to carry on a battle at sea with an enemy having a more modern fleet consisting of better quality ships, manned by more highly trained personnel, and employing tactics which were new for that time. The main result of the victory achieved in the naval engagement was that the home country and the British colonies became practically invulnerable to attacks from the direction of the sea. England was able to deprive the enemy of the weapon which was most dangerous for her—the navy. Only a navy at that time could directly threaten the home country and the security of the communications connecting England with the colonies which supplied the raw materials for her industry and food products for the population. The liquidation of the threat from the sea freed the hands of the English bourgeoisie to organize and finance new alliances to continue the struggle with Napoleonic France. France, however, was forced to refrain once and for all from combat operations at sea and to seek other ways not connected with the sea to combat her main enemy.

Thus, the course of the war at sea and the gaining of domination by the English Navy had a great effect on the further policy of the belligerents.

From all that has been said, it follows that from the dawning of the capitalist era, the navies of the Western states have represented not only a part of the armed forces, which were employed in war in the naval theaters, but also a weapon of state policy in peacetime, which permitted them to enslave underdeveloped peoples and countries overseas and to transform them into their own colonies. The fleets of the Western European powers travelled the path from "privateers in the service of the King" to regular naval forces which received an organized structure and official operational tactics. The employment of this naval force in wars, especially when it was the main force in achieving the goals of the war, had a considerable influence on state policy, which was determined and conducted taking into account the disposition of the forces at sea at certain times.

Maritime states having great economic capabilities have widely used their naval forces in peacetime to put pressure on their enemies, as a type of military demonstration, as threats of interrupting sea communications, and as a hindrance to ocean commerce.

Navies have served these states as an important means of further enrichment and of extending expansion and colonization.

In addition, navies have also carried out the pleasant mission of being discoverers. Naval ships of the great powers, including Russia, have carried out wide-scale oceanographic studies and have made an inestimable contribution to the science of geography. This tradition of mariners (including also naval mariners) still continues even today, when the "blank spots" in the ocean are becoming fewer and fewer, yet the knowledge of the secrets of the ocean represents a very great scientific task even today.

CHAPTER SIX

Sailing the Global Commons

The term "global commons" is now part of the regular naval lexicon. Four decades ago it was less commonly used but its purpose, to describe those areas of the world beyond the control of any single state or political body, free for use by all for the common good, would undoubtedly have been understood. It means, amongst other things: the high seas, the landmass of Antarctica, the atmosphere, and today, space and cyberspace.

It comes as no surprise, then, that in his final article in the "Navies in War and Peace" series, Gorshkov turned his attention to the challenges and opportunities posed by this maritime no-man's-land. Of course, much of his language was politically biased but that does not necessarily lessen the power or contemporary relevance of his ideas. Limiting ourselves to the familiar Anglo-American, "Western" outlook results in an unnecessarily narrow interpretation of global issues. Getting inside the 1970s Soviet perspective helps us to understand the world as seen through Russian, Chinese, Indian, or even multinational corporation eyes today. And learning another language has the beneficial side effect of better understanding our own.

To a geopolitical warrior like Gorshkov it made no sense to either ignore the high seas, what he called the World Ocean, or to leave their exploration and exploitation to others, especially the enemies of the Soviet Union. He saw how the capitalist West was using the sea and concluded that the maritime environment was no longer primarily a means of communication but, increasingly, a provider of resources. Resources usually lead to competition, competition to conflict, and conflict (sometimes) to war. Gorshkov's message, which in the early pages of this article echoes Mahan, was about the need for states to consider areas of the high seas as part of their wider sphere of influence, if not always under their direct, tight control. Chinese activity in and around the South China Sea is a twenty-first-century manifestation of this long-established strategy.

He dedicated some time to discussing the "chemistry" of the oceans—by which he meant their physical composition, oceanography, and economic potential—and addressed the vexing issue of legal claims to ownership and use. Gorshkov saw no justification for states to claim territorial limits of any more than twelve miles; he advocated continental shelf limits based on a combination of depth and distance from shore, and he was a keen supporter of the right of innocent passage for warships and of overflight through international straits for aircraft. Of course, his arguments were timely and were published during the period of negotiations for the third United Nations Convention on the Law of the Sea (UNCLOS), which began in 1973. Ultimately, the USSR signed UNCLOS; the United States is yet to ratify it.

Clearly, his words would not have been entirely altruistic: he was aware that nominal allies of the West had made claims on large areas of the sea and the seabed, and he had personal experience in the difficulties associated with international straits, particularly the restrictions that the USSR felt when trying to move its Black Sea Fleet to the Mediterranean through the Bosporus and Dardanelles. If he had been alive, one wonders how he would have reacted to the dropping of a titanium tube containing a Russian flag from a manned submersible at the North Pole in 2007. It was, of course, part of a play for influence and "ownership" of the High North. Twenty-first-century Chinese adventurism in the South and East China Seas raises other equally interesting and challenging dilemmas, as does India's desire to be the master of the Indian Ocean.

Taking his stance on the moral high ground further, Gorshkov also argued against any attempts to weaponize the seabed. At the time he was undoubtedly concerned about the development of underwater sensors in the Greenland-Iceland-UK gap and the Northern Pacific and the effect that they would have on the Soviet ability to conduct the submarine operations that had become the backbone of the Red Fleet. Self-interest is a difficult vice to shake, if it is a vice at all. Gorshkov, a declared internationalist (but also a fervent nationalist), also argued against the creation of supra-national institutions that could regulate activity and act as umpires on rival claims to maritime exploitation. His concern, he stated, was that due to the workings of the international capitalist market, those institutions would inevitably be run by the very states that he saw as the greatest offenders against the integrity and freedom of the global commons.

In the second part of his article, Gorshkov introduced navies into this complex geopolitical problem, maintaining that they had a vital role to play. First, they were an integral part of the tapestry that led to greater understanding of the maritime environment, from hydrographic survey and weather reporting to the monitoring of patterns of life. Second, through their own activity, they could affirm the principles of freedom of navigation. Third, they could protect others going about their lawful business. And, fourth, they could act as forward-deployed instruments of their states and prevent any other single or group of actors from dominating the oceans. To do this, the navy in question needed to be supported and enabled by a credible merchant marine, a shipbuilding and ship repair industry, and a global network of ports it could rely on. Today, many question the purpose and relevance of navies in a globalized world; in 1974 Sergei Gorshkov gave a rational and level-headed answer that still applies.

The final part of the article—the conclusion to the whole "Navies in War and Peace" series—reads at times like a love letter to Soviet sailors everywhere. (Perhaps it was—Gorshkov was not averse to playing to his audience.) He made the point that no matter how technologically advanced a navy was, and he was obviously proud of the Soviet navy's technological accomplishments, its foundation was always the sailor. To act as guardian and guarantor of the global commons navies needed to be out there, and that meant long deployments and long periods of separation for sailors and their families. Gorshkov acknowledged this and the importance of morale to the missions at hand. Communications with home, psychological preparation (including political indoctrination), training, good leadership, and experience were all amongst his essential ingredients.

Taken together it was, and remains, a convincing approach. Gorshkov certainly did not have a narrow view of naval power and he was keenly aware of the importance of the environment, the law, precedent, accepted norms, and human nature. His ideas undoubtedly had their roots in the classic works of Mahan and others, but they were honed to the time and place in which he operated. Today's (and tomorrow's) maritime strategies, whether they be for national defense or commercial exploitation, regional hegemony or global cooperation, must similarly re-evaluate enduring assumptions and test them against contemporary challenges. "Navies in War and Peace" offers one example of how this was done when the Red Navy was sailing the global commons.

NAVIES IN WAR AND PEACE

U.S. Naval Institute *Proceedings*, 1974

Some Problems in Mastering the World Ocean

In analyzing the essence of imperialism, Vladimir Illich Lenin pointed out that financial capital, afraid of lagging behind in the furious struggle for the still underdeveloped parts of the world, is striving to seize as many different expanses of the globe as possible, assuming that they will later on become a source of raw materials. Areas of the earth which are unsuited

---

Sergei Georgiyevich Gorshkov, "Navies in War and Peace," U.S. Naval Institute *Proceedings* 100, no. 11 (November 1974), pp. 54–67.

for exploitation today, V.I. Lenin noted, may become suitable tomorrow in connection with the incredibly rapid growth of technical progress, which will permit finding new methods of exploiting them and extracting profits.

In the 18th and 19th centuries the efforts of the largest powers were directed toward the seizure of lands being opened up, their colonization, and later toward the development and re-division of them. At that time the seas and oceans were basically merely the arena for the struggle between enemy navies for control of communications, but were not objects of clashes of state interests.

In recent decades in the era of the exploitation of the resources of the World Ocean, an ever increasing struggle has begun between imperialist countries for the division of it for economic and military aims, since it is becoming an immediate objective of their expansion. It is quite evident that navies, as an instrument of policy of the aggressive states, will not be able to take a back seat in this struggle.

The level and tempo of the development of science and technology in the context of today's scientific-technical revolution are creating vast possibilities for the study, mastery, and use of the World Ocean and its bottom for practical economic and military purposes. Therefore, attempts are already being made by certain capitalist states to usurp individual areas of it and to divide up spheres of influence in it. Thus, voices are being heard in the U.S. Congress calling on Americans to move to the East and by 1980 to occupy the Atlantic Ocean bottom up to the Mid-Atlantic Ridge, for, according to the authors of these statements, when it is a question of the ocean bottom, no one mentions borders: He who takes, is right. A highly alarming symptom is the practice by certain states of expanding the limits of their territorial sea up to 200 miles, which is nothing other than an attempt to seize great expanses of the ocean.

The main reason for the level of interest by states in the World Ocean is its truly inexhaustible resources, while the aggressive powers are attracted by its vast military significance.

As is well known, sea water contains all the elements of Mendeleyev's periodic system; the total amounts of these minerals reach fantastic figures. According to calculations by scientists the ocean water has some 10 million tons of gold, four billion tons of uranium, and 270 billion tons of heavy water. The reserves of metals, minerals, fuels (oil, gas, and coal), various chemical raw materials, nuclear material, power and food reserves, locked in the seabed, are so vast that there is no comparison whatsoever with the known reserves existing on land.

A considerable part of the seabed is covered with ore nodules consisting of iron, manganese, cobalt, nickel, copper, and rare earth elements. Geologists believe that great reserves of various natural resources lie in the seabed. Already major deposits of oil and gas are known today in the North Sea, in the Gulf of Mexico, in the Persian Gulf, off the coasts of Alaska and California, and in other areas. Moreover, it is postulated that the main deposits of oil and gas are located not on land but in the seabed. And although mankind will be able to utilize fully all of these riches only in the future, the importance of exploiting them is already increasing today. Prospecting for oil and gas reserves is being carried out in almost all of the areas of the continental shelf, and the output of "maritime" oil is approaching 20% of the entire petroleum output. The truly inexhaustible energy resources of the ocean—its tides, currents, temperature gradients of the water, etc.—also are of vast economic interest.

The reserves of animal protein, i.e., fish, sea animals, plankton, etc., in the World Ocean (if measures are taken to restock them) make it possible to consider it to be one of the most important sources for solving the food problem for the growing population of the world. Today, the catching of fish and other "gifts of the sea" is carried out only in a small part of the ocean surface, consisting of about 10% of it. The annual world catch of fish equals some 60 million tons, but in the near future it may reach 100 million tons or more.

The basic problem of "sea chemistry" arising in practice is the extraction of rare earth and trace elements from the waters. The problem of obtaining common salt, magnesium, bromine, potassium, iodine, and several other substances from sea water has been successfully solved from an economic and technical standpoint; ways have been found to obtain uranium, gold, and other valuable elements from sea water. The dimensions and scale of this work are such that in the near future major changes may be produced in the world economy.

The attack on the ocean is underway on an expanded front. Today man is capable of living and working at depths down to 200 meters and soon undersea stations will be lowered down to 700–1,000 meters. The bathyscaphe *Trieste* has already dived to a depth of 10,919 meters, reaching the bottom of the Mariana Trench, the deepest known trench in the World Ocean. In the coming decades, a fuller, economically effective utilization of all the resources of the World Ocean, supported by technology, will be realized.

The scale of exploitation of the ocean is characterized by the following data published in the American journal *Foreign Affairs*; in 1956, U.S. expenditures on oceanographic work were 25 million dollars, in 1968 they were 448 million dollars, and in 1970 they increased to 900 million dollars.

The growth in appropriations for these goals, which is being observed on an international scale, is explained by the economic interest of all states in a more complete utilization of the riches of the oceans. Today this is one of the most important international and national problems entering the world political sphere. Just as in the 19th century the question of the division of land into spheres of influence became particularly acute, at the present time the intentions of several capitalist countries to establish spheres of influence in the World Ocean is becoming no less acute. The imperialist states are no longer restricting themselves by their own laws concerning the exploitation of the natural resources of the continental shelf: they are striving to extend their national jurisdiction to the open waters of seas and oceans located vast distances from their shores.

Attempts at usurping certain areas of the seabed by individual bourgeois countries are becoming an increasingly blatant and widespread practice, subjugating certain fields of politics, economics, production, and science. And inevitably contradictions and crisis situations arise here. Thus, some countries, in carrying out the development and surveying of the continental shelf, are already raising the question of prohibiting freedom of navigation and the cruising of naval ships in the waters over the locations of undersea work, the question of a significant expansion of the territorial sea, etc. The posing of this question in this way is having a definite effect on the status of the high seas and freedom of navigation, which are the main legal instruments ensuring the regulation of the mutual relations between sovereign states whose interests come into contact with one another in the international waters of the World Ocean.

The CPSU program calls for not only the utilization of known natural resources, but also prospecting for new ones. The World Ocean is assuming extreme importance in connection with this. The study of it and utilization of resources is becoming one of the most major state problems aimed at supporting the economic might of the Soviet Union. A great deal of attention was paid to this in the documents of the 24th CPSU Congress and in the speeches of the delegates. In a report to the 24th Party Congress, Secretary General of the CPSU Central Committee L. I. Brezhnev said: "Our country is ready to participate together with other interested states in the solution of such problems as . . . the study and mastery of space and of the World Ocean."

However, this is possible only if the bottom of the seas and oceans remains a sphere of peaceful cooperation and if it will not be seized by the imperialists and transformed into a bridgehead for the emplacement of new forms of weapons.

Scientific technical progress has permitted man to master parts of the planet, the sea and ocean bottoms, which until recently were inaccessible. Yet at the same time this process also created the prerequisites for positioning of nuclear and other forms of mass destruction weapons there by aggressors. This is why peace loving states, headed by the Soviet Union, are waging a struggle against a new arms race, so that the seabed will remain a sphere of peaceful international cooperation. The treaty prohibiting the locating of nuclear or other forms of mass destruction weapons on or under the seabed, concluded at the initiative of the Soviet Union, has become the first, but important, step on the path to solving this question. This treaty encompasses all areas of the World Ocean located beyond the 12-mile limit of the coastal zone of the territorial sea. The treaty, which was signed by more than 90 states, went into force on 18 May 1972.

A definite impact on the division of the ocean was made by the signing in 1958 of the Geneva Convention on the Continental Shelf according to which all littoral states were granted the right of ownership of the resources of the seabed in their own sections of the shelf down to a depth of 200 meters or beyond this limit to a point at which the water depth permits exploitation of the resources of this area. A defect in the Convention is the absence of a clear-cut wording concerning the outer limits of the continental shelf of the littoral states. This vagueness makes it possible for certain capitalist states to seek ways of seizing vast areas beyond the limits of the shelf.

Today the serious threat of a further division of the World Ocean exists. Therefore, it is not by chance that many countries and a great number of international organizations, beginning with the U.N. and ending with dozens of different types of intra-governmental and nongovernmental organizations and organs, are engaged with questions of the legal regime and with the development of new norms regulating the use of the World Ocean. The most characteristic feature in their work in the current stage is the fact that several AfroAsian and Latin American developing countries are insisting on a review of all existing standards, regulating the use of the World Ocean, based on the fact that they did not participate in their exploitation. In particular, they assert that current international maritime law is outmoded and does not reflect changes which have occurred in the world since 1958. Representatives of these countries put their position on the plane of a struggle between the poor and rich, the backward and the industrially developed countries, which, according to their assertions, are putting national interests first.

The delegations of the U.S.S.R. or other Socialist countries have sharply criticized such extremist views at the United Nations, pointing out that such a nonclass-oriented approach, i.e., the simple division of people into rich and poor, was not only unjust, but also was deeply in error and insulting to the peoples of Socialist countries. They have created their own wealth themselves, without exploiting anyone, while the imperialist powers have profited from the exploitation of colonial peoples. That is why they must be required to return at least a part of what was stolen to the developing countries.

In order to prepare proposals concerning many problems of international maritime law, an expanded U.N. Committee on the Peaceful Use of the Seabed Beyond the Limits of National Jurisdiction was created and is in operation. In accordance with General Assembly Resolution 2750c (XXV) of 17 December 1970, it was transformed into an organ for preparing for an international conference on maritime law. At the 27th Session of the U.N. General Assembly a resolution was adopted concerning the holding of two sessions of the conference in 1973–1974. Various legal aspects of the *use* of the World Ocean will be examined in the course of the Committee's work. In connection with this several countries raised the question of a complete review of the existing legal regime of the World Ocean and of the violation of all existing regulations of international maritime law. There are also statements against even freedom of the high seas on the ground that this principle is outmoded and is being used by the imperialists to the detriment of the interests of the developing countries. Our position on this question is very clear. The imperialists' violation of the legal norms attests not to the insufficient effectiveness of *these* norms, but rather to the strengthened aggressiveness of imperialism itself, which is stressed in the decisions of the 24th CPSU Congress. Therefore, it is not the norms themselves which must be changed but, above all, cooperation must be achieved between peace-loving forces in order to force the imperialists to strictly observe existing regulations.

Several, developing countries are steadily promoting the idea of developing a convention on the seabed regime and on creating an international organ with very extensive powers which would become, essentially, a supranational organ and would control all exploitation of the seabed conducted by different countries. It is quite evident that such an approach is not very realistic, since it actually envisions an institution of *some* sort of international consortium in which inevitably, due to the objective laws of the capitalist market, the largest imperialist monopolies would play the main role. Therefore, regardless of the good intentions of the authors of this idea, the power in the organization would belong to precisely those forces which its creation is supposed to protect against.

The attention of international organs concerned with the *use* of the World Ocean is riveted today on the question of the breadth of the territorial sea. Experience has shown the viability of a 12-mile limit for the breadth of the territorial sea. Presently 54 states have 12-mile territorial seas, 26 have 3-mile limits, 10 states have 4- and 6-mile seas, four states have 30-mile limits, two have 80-mile territorial seas, there are single states with 10, 18, 100, and 130 mile territorial seas. Eight Latin American and one African state have 200-mile territorial seas. Experts have calculated that if all countries declared a 200-mile territorial sea, then of the 360 million square kilometers of water on our planet, about 140–150 million square kilometers would be appropriated by the coastal states. Almost all of the seas would be transformed into their territorial seas and, in particular, the Mediterranean would turn out to be completely divided up.

The key to the solution of this question is the strict establishment of limitations on the breadths of territorial seas, since a further extension could create the danger of an actual division of the high seas. Such a danger is already taking shape today, if you consider scientific technical progress and the modern means and practical capabilities which states presently have at their disposal. Based on existing practice, and on a sensible combination of interests of the coastal states with the principles of the freedom of the high seas, it would *seem* completely acceptable to limit the breadth of the territorial sea to limits of up to 12 miles.

The problem of the innocent passage of combatants and auxiliaries and aircraft overflights through international straits is also a subject of discussion. A considerable number of U.N. delegations believe that freedom of the high seas is unthinkable without freedom of navigation through international straits connecting the high seas and oceans which have long served mankind as important peaceful waterways.

Many sea powers, and also countries not having access to the sea, are expressing concern that even with the adoption of a 12-mile limit for the breadth of the territorial sea, more than 110 straits being used for international shipping will turn out to be closed territorial seas of littoral states. It is evident that this may have a considerable *effect* on the legal status of those straits which until now have been part of the high seas and which have been used for navigation without any sort of limitations. Therefore, in those straits which connect the open seas and are used for international shipping, all transiting ships (and in the wider straits also aircraft flying overhead) must be accorded equal freedom of transit and over-flight.

Concrete proposals were introduced on freedom of navigation in straits by the Soviet Union at the fourth session of the U.N. Committee on the Seabed. In particular it is envisaged that in narrow straits, littoral states will be able to establish appropriate corridors for the transit of ships through straits and for aircraft overflights of the straits. These proposals do not affect the legal regime of those straits through which passage is regulated by special international agreements.

And there is one more problem provoking sharp discussions—the definition of the outer limit of the continental shelf. The positions of states on this question are extremely diverse. Thus, the U.S.A. is advocating the concept of a 200-meter depth for the outer limit of the shelf. However, this concept is not finding widespread support from a majority of the developed and developing countries. Indonesia and Cyprus are expressing concern with regard to the fact that the establishment of a single criterion for determining the outer limit of the shelf would lead to injustice and inequality between states: one would have a large shelf, and others would not have one at all. Therefore, they propose defining the limit of the shelf taking into account both depth and distance from shore. Mexico and Australia, for example, consider the regulations of the 1958 Convention on the

Continental Shelf completely sufficient. There are also other proposals, however; an analysis of them shows that a more realistic limit would be one which would be established taking into account the criteria of depth and distance from shore.

Many countries are insisting on a rapid determination of the shelf limit, since the danger exists of certain states declaring vast areas of the seabed to be their own shelf, and many countries are coming out for adoption of criteria for establishing shelf limits acceptable to all states.

The above questions far from cover the list of problems connected with the use of the World Ocean attracting the attention of practically all states and constantly in the realm of international negotiations being conducted on different levels by different departments. The number of such problems is not decreasing and continues to grow. One of them raised by the Soviet Union and other Socialist countries is the prohibition of using the seabed for military purposes. This was raised because of the fact that in several capitalist countries, development of programs for building undersea equipment for the militarization of the ocean bottom at great depths is proceeding on a broad front. The statements of a prominent figure in the U.S. military circles published in the journal *Foreign Affairs* attest to the true intentions of the American imperialists in regard to the World Ocean: "In ten years or so we shall begin to carve out sections of the ocean far from shore which will be important to us from the point of view of our national defense. And we shall prohibit access by any other country to the areas staked out by us."

Everything that has been said above attests to the importance of the treaty prohibiting the placing of dangerous forms of weaponry on the seabed or under it, signed on 11 February 1971. Moreover, it is difficult to overestimate the significance of this treaty both as a measure to limit the expansionist desires of individual states, and as a first step on the path toward complete demilitarization of the seabed leading to the cessation of the ruinous and wasteful arms race.

The Problems of a Modern Navy

In taking into account the importance of questions related to the strengthening of the country's defense from the direction of the sea, the Soviet Union, in cooperation with the other Warsaw Pact member nations, is constantly strengthening her own sea power, including several necessary components.

In order to exploit the World Ocean and to utilize its resources, it is essential to have detailed and comprehensive knowledge of the hydrosphere of the Earth, to understand the processes occurring in it, and its effect on the land and the atmosphere, and on the formation of weather. Knowledge ensuring navigational safety in the oceans and seas and flights over them is also needed. Moreover, reliable information on the various resources existing in the hydrosphere and on possible methods of exploiting them is necessary. Special expeditionary, research oceanographic ships, scientific organizations, equipment, and, of course, the appropriate personnel are required to understand the seas and oceans. All of this is one component of the sea power of a country.

Our country, its scientists, and navymen have written many glorious pages in the history of geographic discoveries and seafaring, and in the ocean sciences. We are presently conducting a large volume of research on the hydrosphere. Yet the World Ocean still remains the least studied section of the globe, and the scale of work on trying to understand it must and will be expanded in the future.

An important integral part of sea power is the equipment and personnel which make possible the practical utilization of the oceans and seas as transport routes connecting continents, countries, and peoples. For this it is essential to have a merchant marine, a network of ports and services supporting its operation, and a developed shipbuilding and ship repair industry. In 1972, the Soviet Merchant Marine, which is growing at a rapid rate, was sixth among the merchant fleets of the world. A majority of its ships have been built in recent years and are among the more technically advanced ships.

The next component of sea power is the ships, technical equipment, and personnel needed for the practical exploitation and utilization of the resources of the World Ocean, i.e., the fishing fleet. Today our country has the strongest fishing fleet in the world at its disposal. The sea and ocean fishing industry will be developed even further, will exploit new areas, and will expand the assortment of products of the sea being caught. The broadest prospects are opening up in the creation of equipment for extracting mineral resources from the water, from the sea bottom, and from beneath it.

However we must consider the most important component of the sea power of the state to be the Navy, whose mission is to protect state interests on the seas and oceans and to defend the country from possible attacks from the direction of the seas and oceans.

Through the efforts of the people in the Soviet Union a nuclear missile, technically advanced Navy has been created as an indispensable integral part of the Soviet Armed Forces.

The need to have a powerful Navy corresponding both to the geographical position of our country and to its political importance as a great world power has already long been understood, as we have said above. However, this question became particularly acute in the post-war years, when as a result of the alignment of forces in the world arena, the U.S.S.R. and other Socialist countries found themselves surrounded on all sides by a hostile coalition of maritime states posing the serious threat of a nuclear missile attack from the direction of the sea.

At the same time the imperialists, headed by the U.S.A., having created a situation for the Socialist countries in which they were surrounded from the direction of the sea, did not experience a similar danger. Could the Soviet Union reconcile itself to such a situation? Could it agree to an age long domination of the seas and oceans by the traditional western sea powers, especially under the conditions when vast areas of the oceans had become launching pads for nuclear missile weaponry?

Of course not!

The Communist Party and the Soviet government fully appreciated both the threat to our country which is arising from the oceans, and the need to deter the aggressive aspirations of the enemy through the construction of a new, ocean going Navy. And this need is being answered.

While continuing a policy of peaceful co-existence between different social systems and of prevention of a new world war, our Party and government are taking serious steps to ensure the security of the Socialist countries. The chief measure was the building up of powerful modern Armed Forces, including the Navy, capable of opposing any enemy plots, also including those in the oceanic sectors, where the mere presence of our Fleet presents a potential aggressor with the need to solve those same problems himself which he had hoped to create for our Armed Forces.

The need to build a powerful ocean going Navy, which stemmed from the situation which arose on the oceans in the post-war period, from the policy of the U.S.S.R., and from her military doctrine, was backed up and is being backed up by the vast capabilities of the military-economic potential of the Soviet state and by the achievements of our science and technology.

In speaking of the military economic potential of our country, it should be noted that it possesses vast, practically inexhaustible energy, raw material, and fuel resources. The high, stable rate of growth of the economic power of the U.S.S.R., observed throughout its entire history, confirms the stability, planned nature, and harmoniousness of the process of development of the Soviet state.

The utilization of the achievements of science and industry together with the introduction of scientific methods in determining the more valuable mix of weapons and equipment characteristics, taking into account economic factors, has made it possible for naval development to approximate the Navy's vital needs to the maximum degree, without copying naval construction in the Western countries and following our own national path which best corresponds to the specific tasks facing the Navy and the conditions for carrying them out.

The operational combat qualities of the new weaponry, of the means for depicting the situation, and of power plants, have been an important precondition determining the development of the Soviet Navy. Here, nuclear weaponry, which has permitted the Navy's submarine forces to become a part of the country's strategic nuclear forces, should be considered the decisive factor.

The ballistic missiles of submarines have ensured the capability of destroying strategic targets of the enemy deep in his territory from different directions.

Cruise missiles have become a most important weapon for destroying surface targets. Their appearance has introduced radical changes in the organization of a naval engagement and permits the delivery of powerful and accurate attacks from great ranges against the enemy's major surface ships.

Shipboard sea-to-air missiles together with automatic antiaircraft guns are the main means of ship air defense.

Electronics have had a great influence on the trend of naval construction. The employment of electronics has increased ship and aircraft capabilities to destroy surface targets. The use of electronics has sharply improved the efficiency of air reconnaissance, has opened up great possibilities for increasing the depth of the air defense system for surface ships, and supports their effective employment of surface-to-air missiles for self-defense.

Nuclear power, being an inexhaustible power source for long range ship cruises, is greatly increasing their combat capabilities. However, these qualities, which are new in principle, are being imparted only to submarines, which are being transformed into genuine undersea warships, incorporating in themselves such basic earmarks of sea power as maneuverability, hitting power, and concealment. Submarines are also becoming valuable antisubmarine combatants, capable of detecting and destroying the enemy's missile carrying submarines.

The equipping of submarines with nuclear power plants has made possible a sharp increase in the speed and range of their underwater navigation. And this is understandable, since the power-to-weight ratio of submarines with a nuclear power plant considerably surpasses that of diesel submarines.

The above-cited qualities of the new weaponry, means for depicting the situation, and nuclear power are greatly increasing the combat capabilities of all the forces of the Navy. They are objectively fostering the advance of submarines and aviation into the forefront of these forces. This also accounts for the general priority development of submarines and aviation within the navies of the great powers.

Military geographical conditions, which even today the imperialists strive to utilize primarily in order to surround the Socialist countries with a ring of their naval and air bases and also with groupings of naval forces, have always had an important influence on naval development. In peacetime, the imperialists have deployed these groupings in combat patrol areas ready to deliver a surprise attack against land objectives located on the territory of the Soviet Union and of the countries of the Socialist community. According to the testimony of the Americans themselves, the U.S.A. alone has 3,429 military bases, and supply and administrative points manned by 1.7 million men in various countries outside its national borders.

The process of the approach of U.S. bases toward the borders of the U.S.S.R. is continuing, despite the measures taken by the Soviet government to ease international tensions and despite the SALT talks. We cannot be indifferent to the creation of a new naval base for the Sixth Fleet in Greece—in direct proximity to the territory of the People's Republic of Bulgaria and within carrier aircraft range of the central regions of the Soviet Union. We also cannot remain indifferent to the expansion of the basing of U.S. nuclear powered submarines and carrier forces on the Japanese islands, in Italy (Maddalena Island), in the Indian Ocean, and in other areas of the World Ocean, for all of this powerful and widely dispersed military organization is directed against the U.S.S.R. and the countries of the Socialist community.

Naturally these circumstances—and the military-geographical conditions and operational combat qualities of the new weapons and equipment—have had an effect on the building of our Navy, whose combatants, both with respect to design and with respect to armament, differ significantly from the warships of the Western states.

As is well known, through the will of the CPSU Central Committee a course has been charted in our country toward the construction of an ocean going Navy whose base consists of nuclear powered submarines of various types. It is precisely these forces, combining in themselves the latest achievements of scientific-technical progress, which are characterized by such qualities as great endurance and high combat capabilities.

However, a modern navy, whose mission is to conduct combat operations against a strong enemy, cannot be only an undersea navy. The underestimation of the need to support submarine operations with aircraft and surface ships cost the German high command dearly in the last two wars. In particular, we have already pointed out above that one of the reasons for the failure of the "unlimited submarine war" prosecuted by the Germans was the absence of such support for the submarines, which forced them to operate alone without the support of other forces.

Therefore, we, while giving priority to the development of submarine forces, believe that we have a need not only for submarines, but also for various types of surface ships. The latter, in addition to giving combat stability to the submarines, are intended to accomplish a wide range of missions both in peacetime and in war. The diversity of the tasks confronting us has evoked the need to build numerous types of surface ships with a specific armament for each of them. It is characteristic that the attempts which have been made in many countries to build general purpose combatants to carry out all (or many) missions have been unsuccessful. Therefore surface ships continue to remain the most numerous (with respect to type) of naval forces.

The foreign and domestic preconditions cited above which determined the development of the Navy in the postwar period have had a considerable effect on the formation of views on its role in modern warfare. Thus, in connection with the equipping of the Navy with strategic nuclear weapons, the Navy is objectively acquiring the capability not only of participating in the crushing of the enemy's military economic potential, but also in becoming a most important factor in deterring his nuclear attack.

In this connection, missile carrying submarines, owing to their great survivability in comparison with land-based launch installations, are an even more effective means of deterrence. They represent a constant threat to an aggressor who, by comprehending the inevitability of nuclear retaliation from the direction of the oceans, can be faced with the necessity of renouncing the unleashing of a nuclear war.

Only our powerful Armed Forces capable of blocking the unrestrained expansionism displayed today all over the world by imperialism can deter its aggressiveness. In addition, of course, to the Strategic Missile Troops, it is the Navy which is this kind of force, capable in peacetime of visibly demonstrating to the peoples of friendly and hostile countries not only the power of military equipment and the perfection of the naval ships, embodying the technical and economic might of the state, but also its readiness to use this force in defense of state interests of our nation or for the security of the Socialist countries.

Naturally, the question arises: What must a Navy be in terms of quality and quantity for this?

Today, in the context of the possible use of new means of combat in naval warfare, and above all of nuclear missile weaponry with various types of carriers, the relative strength of naval forces cannot be measured in numbers of combatants or their total displacements, just as one cannot measure their combat might by the weight of the gun projectile salvoes or by the quantity of torpedoes or missiles being launched.

Today the criterion of comparability of naval capabilities is the relative strength of their combat might calculated by the method of mathematical analysis, by solving a system of multi-criterial problems for various variants of the situation and different combinations of heterogeneous forces and means. This kind of objective analysis permits the determination of the necessary and sufficient composition of forces and the more rational combination of them which we call balanced forces.

Under today's conditions the basic mission of navies of the great powers in a world-wide nuclear war is their participation in the attacks of the country's strategic nuclear forces, the blunting of the nuclear attacks by the enemy navy from the direction of the oceans, and participation in the operations conducted by ground forces in the continental theaters of military operations. In this instance, navies will perform a large number of complex and major missions.

Important missions in protecting the interests of the Soviet state and the countries of the Socialist community confront the Navy in peacetime too.

This latter point is particularly important because local wars, which imperialism is waging practically uninterruptedly, invariably remain within the sphere of imperialist policy. Today these wars can be regarded as a special form of the manifestation of the "flexible response" strategy. By seizing individual areas of the globe and interfering in the internal affairs of countries, the imperialists are striving to gain new advantageous strategic positions in the world arena which they need for the struggle with Socialism and in order to facilitate carrying out missions in the struggle with the developing national freedom movement. Therefore local wars can be regarded as a manifestation of the more determined imperialist methods for acting against the movement for national independence and progress. Under certain circumstances such actions carry with them the threat of escalation into a world war.

The constant upgrading of its readiness for immediate combat operations in the most complex situation is a most important precondition determining the development of the Navy. At the present time, when in a matter of minutes it is possible to reach major strategic targets and even to accomplish particular missions of the war in certain areas, the need is objectively arising to maintain the highest readiness for naval forces and weaponry. This is a consequence of the effect of the development of naval equipment and weaponry and also of the conditions in which navies have to carry out missions.

In light of what has been said above, the old well known formula—"the battle for the first salvo"—is taking on a special meaning in naval battle under present day conditions (conditions including the possible employment of combat means of colossal power). Delay in the employment of weapons in a naval battle or operation inevitably will be fraught with the most serious and even fatal consequences, regardless of where the fleet is located, at sea or in port.

The new requirements for forces and for the means to support them are also determined by the particular features of the employment of navies in the nuclear era. Therefore these special features can be regarded as still another important precondition having an effect on the trend of development of modern navies.

From this stems such requirements for the development of modern navies as *long cruising ranges for ships at high speeds, a great operating range for aircraft, and the introduction into submarines of nuclear power plants.* Long oceanic cruises require that ships have great endurance and good sea-keeping ability. This in turn has a considerable effect on the dimensions and displacement of combatants, especially of surface ships. The greater the endurance of ships, the longer every grouping can stay out in the ocean and the fewer the ships needed in the fleet inventory.

In addition, the long stay of ships at sea, when the machinery, systems, and propulsion plants are forced to run at high speeds is related to *increasing their service life and reliability.*

The long stay of ships in the ocean, frequently under extreme climatic conditions, is being achieved through habitability standards which permit the officers and men to retain a high combat capability as long as necessary.

It goes without saying that diverse technical equipment plays a leading role in keeping up the crew's physical condition and morale. Yet we must not forget the efficient organization of ship replenishment at sea and of their communications with the Motherland, relatives, close ones, friends, etc.

Long ocean cruises by naval ships present new increased demands on rear services support. The campaign to prolong the endurance of ships without returning to port, ship repairing, and aiding damaged ships at sea is being carried out by powerful mobile rear services, including tenders, repair ships, replenishment ships, oilers, and salvage ships.

Thus, the new form of utilizing naval forces is one of the most important factors in determining technical policy in developing modern naval forces.

Yet, however technically advanced a navy may be, and however powerful the weapons it receives are, the foundation of naval forces will always be man—the master of all means of combat. And the role of man in armed combat, of the specialist masterfully controlling weaponry, machinery, instruments, and apparatus, who is capable of utilizing their capabilities fully, will grow as the Navy develops further. Therefore, men, educated by the Party and devoted to the Socialist Motherland, have always been, are, and will remain the main might of our Navy.

The question of training and forming cadres of Soviet navymen and of tempering them morally and politically is becoming particularly acute and taking on special significance now that the Navy has become completely different, and indeed also since the conditions for cruising have changed in connection with its emergence onto the expanses of the World Ocean. Our ships are at sea for long periods close to the imperialist fleets, and have the opportunity to really evaluate their strong and weak points and to observe not only their actions but also reactions to the change in the international situation.

In this connection, the daily service of naval officers is taking on a qualitatively new character. The conditions under which the daily activities of naval officers proceed are immeasurably more complex, and special responsibility is demanded of them for the performance of missions when cruising far from our own ports, for maintaining ships in constant combat readiness, for training reliable personnel, for inculcating personnel with high morale and combat qualities, and tenacity in overcoming the difficulties of sea duty. In this connection, it should be taken into account that not only has the equipment changed and the ships become more complex than several years ago, but also the activity itself of the Navy has considerably expanded.

The Soviet officer bears a special responsibility to the Party and people for the education and conduct of his subordinates, and for their performance of great and difficult missions on long ocean cruises with high military skill and self-assurance. The success of these cruises is determined not only by the reliability of the equipment and weapons built by Socialist industry, but above all by the outstanding schooling of the crews embodying in themselves a deep conviction of the righteousness of our great cause and a high awareness of their filial duty to the Motherland and to the Communist Party.

This is only a part of the considerably more versatile nature of the Soviet naval officer. The successful cruises of our warships in all areas of the World Ocean serve to confirm that the officers of the Navy possess these qualities.

However these successes would be unthinkable without the daily purposeful leadership of the Navy on the part of the Communist Party and without properly organized Party political work. It is not accidental that our military leaders, officers of all ranks, being deeply aware of and piously carrying out the precepts of V. I. Lenin, consider political work a powerful searchlight lighting the way to victory for the soldier and general, the seaman and admiral. Political work is a special weapon of the Party ensuring the boosting of the combat readiness of the armed forces, including also the Navy, inspiring fighting men to feats, and more than ever it is one of the decisive factors of victory. The current situation demands increased vigilance and readiness for the selfless defense of Socialism by the Soviet armed forces and the fraternal armies of the Socialist countries. Constant high combat readiness is primarily determined by exemplary order in the units and forces, and by our naval forces being in a technical condition permitting them to go into action without delay. In the Navy it requires even more outstanding nautical and special training, complete knowledge of the combat capabilities of the equipment, and the ability to employ it masterfully under any climatic conditions and in various sea states.

All of these qualities do not occur spontaneously. In order to shape them, educational work and intensive training is underway the entire year round in the fleets. Navymen acquire comprehensive knowledge and the ability to control machinery and systems and complex modern weaponry in training classrooms, on training ranges, and in trainers, aboard ships and in units. Ocean cruises, long deployments, serve as the highest stage of training, the best and only school capable of strengthening the obtained knowledge and skills, and developing them to the level of mastery.

With the emergence of our ships into the oceans, the Navy acquired the capability of not only completely eliminating arbitrary conditions in combat training and of conducting it under conditions close to actual conditions, but also to thoroughly study that specific feature of the situation in which he will have to perform missions in war, should the aggressors unleash it. Ocean cruises are a school of moral, political and psychological training of personnel for modern warfare. Indeed, it is not as easy as it may seem at first glance in the training process to educate officers, petty officers, and nonrated men in tenacity in achieving goals, initiative, and self-control. These qualities cannot be developed behind a school desk— steadfast, purposeful work is needed on ocean cruises where Navymen are taught to perform their duties in storms and amid the elements, in cold and heat, in fog, and in foul and clear weather. They gain confidence in the reliability of combat equipment and skills in the best employment of it. Long cruises and exercises permit developing the teamwork of the entire crew of the ship, upgrading its schooling, and making sure that the actions of each member of the crew are automatic.

Propaganda concerning revolutionary and combat traditions greatly aids the education of skillful and courageous Navymen. From examples of the military feats, bravery, and courage of the heroes of the Revolution, and the Civil and Great Patriotic Wars, the fighting men learn military skills, the overcoming of difficulties and adversity, and the ability to suc-cessfully carry out assigned missions under any conditions, and they are taught to strive to imitate the heroes of past battles and cruises, and develop the desire to repeat their feats today.

The rich experience of the Great Patriotic War and the postwar long cruises attest to the fact that the Soviet Navyman, inspired by the high ideals of Communism, is capable of overcoming all hardships on cruises and in battle. More than once he has given his life without hesitation for an idea, for in the moment when the heat of the struggle is greatest, ideas have been placed above everything for him, above any hardships. There is no doubt that also in the decisive moments in the future the Soviet Navyman will act precisely as the interests of the Motherland and the interests of the victory of Socialism and Communism demand.

In conclusion, we must say the following.

In order to ensure the defense of a country and the accomplishment of military-political missions, states have always strived to have armed forces appropriate to these aims, including naval forces, and to maintain them at a modern level. Within the armed forces of a country navies fulfill an important role as one of the instruments of state policy in peacetime, and are a powerful means of achieving the political goals of an armed struggle in wartime.

History shows that the creation of major navies is feasible only for maritime states having the necessary resources and a developed economy at their disposal. In this connection, a policy taking into account the country's need for sea power is an important factor determining the nature of naval construction, promoting the mobilization of its capabilities for the indicated goal, and is an indispensible condition of the development of sea power.

An analysis of the alignment of forces in the international arena today and the sharp increase in the capabilities of modern navies to have a decisive effect on all fronts of an armed struggle provide the basis to assert that the absolute and relative importance of naval warfare in the overall course of a war has indisputably grown.

It has been essential in all stages of its history, for our state—a great continental world power—to have a mighty Navy as an indispensible integral part of the armed forces. Today our armed forces have a fully modern Navy equipped with everything necessary for the successful performance of all missions levied upon it on the expanses of the World Ocean.

We must once more stress the fundamental difference in the goals for which the naval forces of the imperialist states, on one hand, and those of the Soviet Union, on the other, have been built and exist. While the navies of the imperialist states are an instrument of aggression and neocolonialism, the Soviet Navy is a powerful factor in the creation of favorable conditions for the building of Socialism and Communism, for the active defense of peace, and for strengthening international security.

The Central Committee of the Communist Party and the Soviet government, in bringing to life the precepts of V. I. Lenin on strengthening the defense of the country, are displaying unwavering attention to boosting the defensive might of the state, to strengthening its armed forces, to increasing its sea power, and to the harmonious, balanced development of the forces of an ocean-going Navy meeting today's needs, and capable of carrying out the tasks confronting them.

L. I. Brezhnev firmly and confidently stated this at the 24th CPSU Congress: "Everything that the people have created must be reliably protected. It is imperative to strengthen the Soviet state—this means strengthening its *Armed Forces,* and increasing the defensive capability of our Motherland in every way. And so long as we live in an unsettled world, this task will remain one of the most primary tasks."

Soviet Navymen consider their highest duty to be the maintenance of a high state of readiness of all naval forces to carry out tasks of defending the state from the direction of the sea, and in every way to improve skills of employing combat equipment under any climatic and weather conditions. All of this must support the protection of the state interests of the Motherland and be a reliable shield from enemy attacks from the sea and a real warning of the inevitability of retaliation for aggression.

The concern of the Communist Party and the Soviet people for the valiant armed forces of the country, including the Navy, serves as a true guarantee of the fact that the Soviet Union will also in the future remain not only one of the strongest continental powers, but also a mighty sea power, a faithful guardian of peace in the world.

CHAPTER SEVEN

The Lessons of History

T his collection has sailed full circle and ends with the topic with which it began. In 1964 the younger Sergei Gorshkov, approaching the zenith of his power over the Soviet fleet and his influence in Moscow, recounted his own experiences in World War II. In the mid-1980s he was a much older man, finally nearing retirement after three decades in command of a world-leading navy, who saw a darker Cold War in train. His writing then, reflecting the times, (mainly) left behind its boasts of communist technological leadership and returned to the subject of the Great Patriotic War. He looked to find solace in the lessons of history that could help the USSR in its current predicament.

Brezhnev had gone. Yuri Andropov, Brezhnev's successor, lasted scarcely two years. Constantin Chernenko, the third old man in quick succession, would hold power for just a year. Afghanistan was taking its toll and, perhaps most importantly, the renewed vigor that Ronald Reagan had brought to Cold War relations, and defense in particular, had left the Eastern bloc on the back foot. The USSR was not yet in total collapse but change was imminent; its economic and political difficulties were only papered over and the cracks were beginning to show. For the navy this meant an outlook significantly different than it had during its earlier era of rapid growth. The Soviet navy is an obvious candidate for analysis when considering the rise of a state's sea power but, equally, it offers lessons of how, and how not, to manage stagnation and relative decline.

Gorshkov left his job as commander in chief of the Soviet navy at the end of 1985 but, before he did, he published two more short articles in *Morskoy Sbornik*. These articles urged a critical analysis of World War II, drawing on the experiences of those who had fought in it whilst they were still alive, to better confront the resurgent United States and NATO in a future promising little but austerity and trouble.

The first of the pair, "Remember the War," which appeared in 1984, was essentially a call to arms. Characteristically, it started with an homage to the Soviet Union and its successes against Nazi Germany and moved quickly to a crude comparison with the United States. He described the ongoing activities of the West as a "massive psychological attack," a proof, if any were needed, of the strategic value of forward presence and cooperative engagement with other like-minded countries. Gorshkov viewed the stationing of American nuclear forces in Europe, a ramping up of NATO military exercises, the U.S. invasion of Grenada, and its policies toward Latin America, with contempt. But he knew they were effective. Gorshkov's underlying point was that the USSR had faced and overcome overwhelming odds before and could do so again.

He was writing his articles to coincide with the fortieth anniversaries of some of the great Soviet milestones of World War II. He specifically mentions the successes of the Black Sea Fleet in the Balkans and the role the Northern Fleet played in the Arctic in 1944. Commanding officers, political workers, engineers, the whole of the navy, he said, must draw on these experiences and apply their lessons to contemporary challenges. However, he warned that they must not do so "mechanically." With the passage of time comes a change in context and circumstance; history rarely repeats itself and Gorshkov did not advocate the study of dry, academic texts. His strategy for learning was a more personal affair, whereby the young would listen to the old. Veterans, he was saying, had a duty in times of need to share their experiences and help to accelerate the "practical conditioning" of those on the modern front line. In "Remember the War" Gorshkov stopped short of identifying any particular lesson to be adopted, but he made clear that others should not.

In the second article, "The Experience of the Great Patriotic War and the Present State of Development of the Naval Art," written a year later and published during his last days as commander in chief, Gorshkov did offer more. That article started with a deeper discussion of Soviet naval successes in World War II, accompanied by plenty of statistics and easy examples of heroic deeds by the various fleets. However, once it settled into its flow it posed a fundamental, albeit rhetorical question: had the experience of previous combat lost its importance to the development of the Soviet navy and wider naval theory? His answer, of course, was emphatically no.

Gorshkov again warned against blindly repeating what may have worked in the past, but this time he outlined some basic principles for the next generation to follow. The Great Patriotic War, he wrote, showed the importance of the relationship between policy and strategy, the "obliteration" of any distinction between theater military operations and the rear, the joint conduct of armed conflict by coalitions, the dependence of military capability on technological progress, and the importance of high morale amongst soldiers and sailors. He presented a list of parameters that would not look amiss in the Gulf in 1991, in Iraq in 2003, in Afghanistan in 2014, or in the fight against Daesh/Islamic State today.

In 1985 the results of those World War II lessons were an oceangoing fleet, a belief in the gods of technology and automation, and a deep-set fear of being the victim of surprise attack. The U.S. Strategic Defense Initiative (Star Wars), for instance, was regarded as part of a first-strike capability belonging to an alliance with a ready appetite for intervention. It is always illuminating to know how others perceive your actions.

In the end it was not a surprise attack by NATO that administered the coup de grâce to the USSR and its navy. It was almost certainly the program of domestic reform instigated by Mikhail Gorbechev in the wake of a crippling and, to Moscow, self-defeating arms race that changed the political landscape. The metamorphosis was beginning as Sergei Gorshkov retired. By the time it reached its conclusion and the Soviet Union was wound up, he was dead. But his ideas remain.

In closing this selection of articles, we must ask ourselves what the true legacy of Sergei Georgiyevich Gorshkov is. He certainly informs us how the outlook of a nation can be transformed in a very short period of time, how it can maintain its continentalism while simultaneously building maritime capability. Twenty-first-century China and India are certainly examples of that. He gives us simple principles to guide us through the process of constructing a navy; how the interplay of geography, technology, civil-military relations, and, of course, people is just as important as platforms. He advocates a much broader view of sea power than the naval element; he explains how scientific research vessels, the merchant marine, fishing fleets, and the extractors of natural resources can cooperate with navies to further national interest. And he provides values and ideas that, though born in the maritime environment, can equally be applied to the other global commons of the twenty-first century.

Finally and most importantly, however, in Gorshkov we have proof that there is always an alternative view. Since the end of the Cold War, perhaps for the past century, Anglo-American concepts of sea power have so dominated that they are accepted in the West almost without question. But unchallenged doctrines become stale dogma and we should never rest on our laurels. A disruptive actor could well undermine maritime superiority before the West has had a chance to observe, orientate, decide, and act. Is that disruptive actor a state, a pseudo-state, or an irregular force bound together by fundamental beliefs? Is that actor with us today?

As the final articles below demonstrate, as the bipolar world drew to a close Gorshkov sought lessons from the formative experiences of World War II. Today, as the uni-polar era comes to an end should we not seek lessons from the experiences of the Cold War, especially while we still have the chance to learn from those who lived it? If we don't, others surely will.

REMEMBER THE WAR

Morskoy Sbornik, 1984

Time passes swiftly, shoving into the past the days when the final shots of the last war died away. But the lessons of history stand before us in greater relief and the effect of victory in the Great Patriotic War on modern times becomes even more clearly visible.

All our thoughts are turned to peace, but the events of those fiery years never will be erased in the people's memory. And the day of our Great Victory will remain the brightest, most memorable and most exciting in the unparalleled military epopee which decided the fate of the Soviet state and world development. It became a bright holiday of Soviet citizens and all freedom loving peoples and an unfading symbol of socialism's inexhaustible vitality.

The path to victory over fascism was long and incredibly difficult. It passed through the fire and blood of numerous battles, the 40th anniversary of which is being celebrated by our entire country.

The Hitlerites' defeat at Moscow, the defense of Leningrad and Sevastopol, the Stalingrad epopee, the Battle for the Caucuses, the clash in the Kursk Bulge, liberation of many European states, the victorious assault on Berlin and the operations which have gone down forever in the history of warfare brought unfading glory to Soviet arms. The Soviet people's heroic struggle under Communist Party leadership, which demonstrated the indisputable advantages of our state and social system and socialist economy and radically altered the course of World War II, had a decisive effect on all postwar development.

The Navy, which fulfilled its duty to the Motherland to the end, made a worthy contribution to the defeat of the hated enemy.

It was then, in the days of heavy fighting against Hitler's invaders, that we dreamed of victory, of peaceful days, and about when the Soviet people would restore the devastated economy and would move on along the path of building a happy socialist life. Today we state with deep satisfaction

Sergei Georgiyevich Gorshkov, "Remember the War," *Morskoy Sbornik,* no. 5 (1984), pp. 5–11.

that the boldest dreams of that time cannot compare with the reality of our days.

The 26th Party Congress and subsequent CPSU Central Committee plenums advanced tasks on a grandiose scale, fulfillment of which will contribute to even greater prosperity for our Motherland and her successful advance along the path of building communism. The Soviet people are working persistently to fulfill the party's historic resolutions.

Their beneficial influence is seen in all spheres of the national economy. The workers' socio-political activeness has significantly increased. Efficiency, planning discipline, and labor discipline are growing. The rhythm of all our life has become more precise. In accomplishing today's tasks Soviet citizens are creating preconditions for achieving higher goals in the future. It was emphasized at the February and April 1984 CPSU Central Committee plenums that the party will strive for deeper qualitative changes in the country's economic and social development and for further improvement in the society of mature, developed socialism.

Our people have to accomplish the creative tasks under difficult foreign policy conditions. A seriously aggravated, explosive international situation is at hand. The reason for this is the aggressive imperialistic policy of the United States and its NATO allies, the edge of which is aimed primarily against the USSR and other countries of the socialist community and against all progressive forces on earth. A number of essential circumstances draw attention to themselves.

While the Soviet Union has not violated and is not planning to violate the approximate military-strategic parity existing between the USSR and United States and between Warsaw Pact and NATO states, the United States is trying with the persistence of one possessed to alter this balance in its favor. Military expenditures of imperialist countries are increasing in an unprecedented manner for this purpose. Washington alone spends $24 million hourly, or $576 million per day, on preparation for war. Qualitatively new weapon systems—nuclear and conventional—are being developed at ever-increasing rates, groupings of armed forces are building up in various parts of the globe and plans for the militarization of space are being worked out.

The Navy holds a significant place in US military preparations. In the opinion of the supreme American leadership, the Navy permits showing up at the door of any coastal state in a short period of time to commit aggression and carry out a "big stick" policy. The new ocean strategy developed by the Pentagon for the 1980s is directed above all against the Soviet Union. The concept of "forward sea lines" became the key to this strategy. By setting up such lines NATO's admirals dream of "turning the Soviets into an isolated island" and forcing our Navy to limit its functions merely to "defense of its own bases."

At the same time Washington is intensively developing submarine-based nuclear forces within the framework of the Trident program and in the current decade is planning to increase the total number of combatants to 600 units, introduce cruise missiles widely, and outfit some 100 surface combatants and submarines with the Tomahawk nuclear missiles. Beginning in 1972 US budget appropriations for development and employment of the Navy have surpassed the expenditures allocated to other branches of the Armed Forces.

From year to year the United States and NATO increase the scale of military exercises, including those in which naval forces participate, simultaneously with the growth in arms. They are conducted over an enormous expanse from the Arctic Ocean to the Mediterranean and the southern latitudes of the Indian and Pacific oceans. In essence this is a rehearsal for unleashing war using both conventional and nuclear missile weaponry.

In conducting a policy of force and crude diktat, American imperialism unceremoniously intervenes in the internal affairs of sovereign states, it is committing impudent piracy in Grenada, Lebanon, Nicaragua, and El Salvador, and it is creating crisis situations in other parts of the world. An explosive situation arises as a result, and not just in individual regions; the threat of nuclear war is growing for the entire world.

Washington is stubbornly drawing other countries into the orbit of military preparations. The US administration is undertaking vigorous efforts to revive Japanese militarism and tie it to NATO's military-political machine. Attempts are being made to animate the ASEAN bloc and give it an aggressive direction against Vietnam, Laos, and Kampuchea.

The United States and NATO have unfolded a massive "psychological" attack against the USSR and other countries of the socialist community for the purpose of preparing broad public opinion for the idea of the alleged inevitability of a struggle against socialism and communism by military means, deceiving nations, and concealing from them the imperialist reaction's true desire for world domination. Hence the conduct of ideological subversion, blackmail, and provocations against socialist states.

The stationing of new American medium-range missiles which has begun in Europe represents extraordinary danger for the cause of peace. "One can only be surprised at the zeal with which certain responsible figures of West European states," emphasized USSR Minister of Defense, Marshal of the Soviet Union D. F. Ustinov at a meeting with veterans in December of last year, "are persistently dragging the American Pershings and cruise missiles into their own 'garden' and are turning the territory of their countries into springboards for a nuclear missile war against the USSR, cloaked in the myth of the 'Soviet military threat' and despite the will of the majority of their own population."[1]

People of the older generation remember well the international situation on the eve of World War II and the Great Patriotic War. They know what disasters the short-sighted policy of connivance with aggressors on the part of certain western powers brought to the world. States of the fascist bloc also at that time concealed their true face with anti-communism and anti-sovietism. Unfortunately some people abroad are closing their eyes to what such a policy today is fraught with.

Having endured the entire burden of the struggle against fascism, the Soviet people cannot forget the lessons of history, and so they are forced to take appropriate retaliatory steps to ensure their own security and the security of their allies.

In connection with the deployment of new American missiles in Europe, the Soviet leadership rescinded the pledges it made on a unilateral basis, which had the purpose of forming more favorable conditions for achieving success in talks on limiting nuclear arms in Europe, including a moratorium on the deployment of Soviet medium-range nuclear weapons in the European part of the USSR.

With consideration of the fact that such actions by the United States increased the nuclear threat for the USSR, corresponding Soviet weapons will be deployed in ocean areas and the seas. These weapons of ours will be adequate in their characteristics to the threat which American missiles being stationed in Europe create for us and our allies.

---

1. *Krasnaya Zvezda*, 15 December 1983.

In taking these forced steps the Soviet state simultaneously is doing everything to divert the danger of war from mankind and normalize the international situation. It has taken and is taking major initiatives of fundamental importance for placing a barrier to a military conflagration which might break out through the fault of imperialism's ultra reactionary forces. It is not because our country has nothing with which to defend itself and its allies that it is conducting the traditional Leninist peace loving policy.

"Let everyone know that no lovers of military adventures will succeed in catching us unawares," said CPSU Central Committee General Secretary, Comrade K. U. Chernenko at a meeting with electors in March of this year, "and no potential aggressor can hope to avoid a crushing retaliatory blow."

We possess sufficient strength to stand up against a military threat. The heroic labor of several generations of the Soviet people created a powerful economic and scientific technical potential—a sturdy material base of the Soviet state's defensive capability and the Armed Forces' combat might.

Thanks to the constant concern of the Communist Party and Soviet government we have in all respects a balanced Navy capable of reliably assuring state interests at sea. Naval forces are undergoing constant development and improvement. Over the last decade the Navy has been augmented by new combatants, equipment, and arms. New strategic nuclear submarines armed with ballistic missiles, as well as multirole submarines, have become part of the submarine forces. Surface forces have been augmented by air-capable ships armed with ship-based aircraft and helicopters and anti-ship missiles. The cruiser *Kirov* with a nuclear power plant and modern missile and antisubmarine weapons became operational. Naval aviation and the naval infantry saw further development.

The Navy's organization and its command and control are being perfected persistently with consideration of the aggravated military-political situation, and battle readiness of ships, units, and forces is improving from day to day.

It can be said boldly that the Navy has ascended to a qualitatively higher level permitting it to accomplish operational training missions with greater effectiveness and to defend our Motherland's state interests in the ocean.

Soviet Navymen also are fulfilling their international duty with honor within the framework of the Warsaw Pact. Ties with allied fleets are constantly growing stronger. People are the Navy's main, deciding force. Officers, warrant officers, petty officers, and seamen brought up by the Communist Party possess political maturity, good professional and technical knowledge, and abundant experience in long ocean deployments and in combat training under difficult conditions. They are infinitely dedicated to the cause of the Leninist Party, the Soviet people, and the building of communism.

Armed Forces personnel are faced with even more responsible missions in connection with the intensification of military danger for our country. Above all it means a further strengthening of vigilance, an increase in readiness to repel aggression no matter where it originates, even greater exertion of efforts in combat and political training, and a strengthening of military discipline.

A steadfast improvement in the military-patriotic indoctrination of Soviet citizens, including Army and Navy personnel, which the party views as an inalienable component of communist indoctrination, is a task of great political and state importance under present-day conditions.

The Navy has accumulated enormous experience in heroic, patriotic work. The activeness of this work rose last year in connection with preparations for and conduct of jubilee celebrations dedicated to the 50th anniversary of the Northern Fleet and the 200th anniversary of Sevastopol. A visit to the Northern and Black Sea fleets by CPSU Central Committee Politburo Member, USSR Minister of Defense, Marshal of the Soviet Union D. F. Ustinov and his presentation of orders to the city-hero Sevastopol and to Murmansk attached special significance to the activities.

The unveiling of the "Combat Glory of the Pacific Fleet" memorial complex, a branch of the Northern Fleet Museum aboard the submarine K-21, and other majestic monuments to Navymen contributed to an intensification of the propaganda of combat traditions.

In arranging heroic patriotic indoctrination the military councils, COs, and political entities direct our cadres' attention above all to imaginative use of the Great Patriotic War's lessons and experience for a further improvement in naval forces under conditions of the specific military strategic situation which has formed in the world.

It is generally known that historical experience teaches a great deal. A knowledge and intelligent use of it is a powerful factor of indoctrinational influence. It contains a concentrated expression of our capabilities, our advantages and our achievements. This experience cautions against a voluntary or involuntary underestimation of military danger being generated by imperialism. It requires looking boldly into the face of military, political realities of contemporary international life and being constantly ready for possible unexpected turns of events, dangerous provocations, and adventures on the part of the most frantic enemies of socialism. In addition, this experience includes the enormous strength of practical example.

At the same time, an imaginative assimilation of the Great Patriotic War's experience must occur with consideration of the contemporary material and technical base of the Soviet Army and Navy and their qualitative growth. New capabilities of arms and equipment permit developing military affairs faster and better and forecasting the nature of a future war, and they improve the Armed Forces' combat might. One must study wartime experience in light of practical missions facing the Navy in order to teach military cadres what is necessary for victory over a strong, well outfitted enemy.

Broad opportunities open up for indoctrinating the personnel in a spirit of allegiance to the Army and Navy's heroic traditions in connection with the upcoming celebration this year of the 40th anniversary of prominent victories by Soviet forces in the largest strategic offensive operations of the Great Patriotic War.

It is apropos to recall that the Navy played an enormous role in battles of the last year of the war. In the latter half of 1944 the Black Sea Fleet successfully cooperated with the Red Army in the Jassy-Kishinev Operation, in defeating the enemy in Romania, and in liberating Bulgaria. The Northern Fleet took an active part in preparing and conducting the Petsamo-Kirkenes Operation in October 1944, which ended with the defeat of Hitlerites in the Arctic and the liberation of Norway. The Baltic Fleet helped our forces in the offensive on the Karelian Isthmus and in the Baltic area. The Danube Naval Flotilla gave support to units which liberated Belgrade, the capital of Yugoslavia, and which operated on the Budapest Axis, and the Dnieper Naval Flotilla distinguished itself in conducting Operation *Bagration*.

The Navy's combat activities to disrupt enemy sea lines of communication and defend our own lines of communication were characterized by high effectiveness.

The 40th anniversary of the enemy's defeat in the Vistula-Oder and Berlin operations and the 40th anniversary of the victorious conclusion of the war against German fascism and Japanese militarism will be celebrated in 1985. Even now we must carefully think out and plan activities devoted to the Great Victory.

The tireless work by Great Patriotic War veterans is truly inestimable in military-patriotic indoctrination. We address words of deep gratitude to the Soviet War Veterans' Committee, its sections, and fleet veterans' councils which bring together thousands of heroes of past battles who are not getting old at heart.

Army and Navy veterans are people of the combat exploit, bearers of high spiritual and moral values of our people, and they are people of enormous military labor both in the stern war years and in peaceful years. They are troubled to the depth of their souls by today's problems of indoctrinating and training personnel and improving combat schooling and the status of battle readiness of the units and ships.

The Navy's present and future depend largely on how young COs, political workers, engineers, and technicians—all personnel—accumulate the experience of older generations and enrich and augment it in practice.

The civic and professional development and maturing of young cadres is advanced to the foreground now. At the present time almost half of the naval officers are under 30 years of age, and their proportion is even higher directly in the forces, aboard ships, and in the units. It is the primary task of those who won victory to pass on to young people their abundant experience and see to it that they receive practical conditioning faster. The famed veterans must share their accumulated experience with older officers as well, especially with COs at all levels, who above all have the responsibility for battle readiness and combat effectiveness of their entrusted forces, ships, and units. This must be done without fail inasmuch as each year there remain fewer and fewer live bearers of invaluable combat experience. The officers must skillfully and firmly command subordinates, direct the activities of party and Komsomol organizations, and constantly rely on them.

Of course, the past war's combat experience must not be transferred mechanically into the present. The years which have passed since then have made their corrections. But there are conclusions of permanent importance which were tested in the flame of battle, which became part of military regulations and military rituals, and which became combat traditions.

It is important for the conclusions based on the varied experience of frontlinesmen and naval veterans to be used as widely as possible in the personnel's operational, tactical, combat, and political training. This work must be activated not just in the period of preparation for banner events; it must be conducted constantly and daily so that more and more generations of Navymen can go along the combat experience as along steps, and not just go, but repeat it and surpass it if necessary.

The work with young Navy people is one of the most important sectors for veterans to apply energy and knowledge. Who if not the people with an enormous store of life experience and whose party or naval term comprises tens of years can help in the ideological, political, military, and moral conditioning of young military men and strengthen their communist conviction and readiness to come to the defense of the socialist homeland at any minute?

Who if not the veterans, telling about their difficult but excellent combat youth, can help those who now have accepted the baton of the Motherland's defenders find the surest paths to military proficiency and convince them of the vital need for strict observance of regulation order and iron military discipline?

The work with young naval people must be arranged so that they gain a profound understanding of the complexity of the military-political situation and the increased threat of war which American imperialism and its accomplices are preparing, and so that, on this basis, they develop an attitude toward the military danger as toward a stern reality of our time and regard fulfillment of their military duty with a high sense of responsibility.

The veterans' assistance to young people of pre-draft age is of great importance in their acquisition of initial military knowledge and skills of military labor and military duty.

We must see to it that each person who prepares to join the ranks of the Motherland's armed defenders has a deep awareness of the high historic purpose of the Soviet Armed Forces and has a clear impression of the Navy's heroic past and present routine and about those ordeals which may fall to his lot should the aggressor dare interrupt our people's peaceful labor.

The June 1983 CPSU Central Committee Plenum re-emphasized the need to improve our propaganda's spirited nature in every way and it demanded giving an offensive character to the fight against the ideology alien to us and instill in military personnel a burning class hatred for the enemies of socialism and peace.

Comrade K. U. Chernenko said at the June 1983 CPSU Central Committee Plenum: "The people rightly call our Army and Navy a school of courage, diligence, and high morality. We must continue to improve the indoctrinational role of the Soviet Armed Forces in every way." This demand of the Communist Party increases the responsibility of COs, political officers, and the party and Komsomol organizations for arranging ideological indoctrination, mass political, and individual work aboard ships and in units; for the entire tenor of military duty; and for the creation of cohesive, united crews and combat collectives in which the rule of life must be: "One for all and all for one."

Today's life and work of the Soviet Army and Navy, like their entire heroic history, are full of examples of exceptional courage, high valor and unbending staunchness. In exercises, on ocean deployments, in long flights, and in performing operational readiness duty everywhere, Soviet military personnel prove themselves to be worthy heirs of the glory of their fathers and grandfathers, continuers of their wonderful traditions.

The training year is in full swing in the Navy. Socialist competition among ships, subunits, and individual servicemen has developed widely under the motto "Be on guard, in constant readiness to defend socialism's achievements!" Each day of combat training brings good news, but we still have many reserves and capabilities for a steady improvement in the effectiveness of military labor and for accomplishing combat and political training missions at a qualitatively higher level.

Our patriotic duty demands this. We are obligated to this by the memory of those who did not return from the front and by lessons of the Great Patriotic War, and we are called to this by Lenin's immortal military precepts.

* * *

The present-day situation demands our constant and comprehensive efforts to ensure national security and reliable protection of Soviet citizens' peaceful labor.

From a speech by Comrade K. U. Chernenko at the April 1984 CPSU Central Committee Plenum

THE EXPERIENCE OF THE GREAT PATRIOTIC WAR
AND THE PRESENT STAGE IN THE DEVELOPMENT OF
THE NAVAL ART

Morskoy Sbornik, 1985

Some four decades separate us, the Soviet people, the peoples of the fraternal socialist commonwealth countries and all progressive mankind, from one of the major world-historical events of the modern age, the victory over Nazi Germany. The Soviet people and their valorous Armed Forces, under the leadership of the Communist Party, dealt crushing defeats to the Nazi invaders, they defended the independence of the homeland of the October Revolution and carried out their international duty in expelling the occupiers from the Eastern European countries, a significant portion of Austria and also freed the German workers from Nazi suppression.

The path to victory was long—1,418 days and nights—and difficult. This war was the fiercest and severest of all the wars which have ever been experienced in the history of our Motherland. Some 20 million sons and daughters of the Soviet Union did not live to see the bright spring day of 9 May.

From the very first day of the treacherous attack by the Nazi hordes on the Soviet Union until the victorious conclusion of World War II in Europe, the Soviet-German Front was the main theater of military operations. Here due to the intentional delay by the United States and England in opening a second front, the Soviet Armed Forces for 3 years fought alone against the crack Nazi troops. It was precisely here that the fate of human civilization was determined. And here the legend of the insurpassability of the military art of the German Army was dissipated like smoke and the myth of the Wehrmacht's invincibility was dispelled.

The defeat of the aggressor was preceded by the enormous organizational work of the Communist Party and the Soviet government during

Sergei Georgiyevich Gorshkov, "The Experience of the Great Patriotic War and the Present Stage in the Development of the Naval Art," *Morskoy Sbornik,* no. 4 (August 1985), pp. 13–22.

the prewar years to strengthen the nation's defense capability, including an increase in its sea power. On the eve of the Great Patriotic War, the Navy represented an impressive force. It included the Northern, Red Banner Baltic, Black Sea and Pacific Fleets as well as the Caspian, Danube, Pinsk and Amur Naval Flotillas. The Navy had 276 combatants of the main classes. In terms of the main tactical and technical specifications, many of them were the equal of analogous foreign ships and even surpassed them in certain areas.

Along with organizing the forces and means for naval warfare, a new Soviet naval theory was developed on the basis of Marxist-Leninist methodology and the recent achievements of military science. Inadequately reflecting the potential combat capabilities of the then modern material base, this theory elaborated concepts of strategic and operational-tactical employment of the naval forces. For the first time in the world an ordered theory of operational art was created and its provisions were the basis for the guidelines of that period, the Provisional Regulation on the Conduct of Sea Operations (NMO-40) and the Field Manual of the RKKA (Worker-Peasant Red Army) Naval Forces (BUMS-37). Running as a constant theme through these was the demand to constantly seek out and in any situation decisively attack the enemy.

A clear system was worked out and put into effect for shifting the naval forces to higher states of alert and these met the military-political conditions actually developing in the theaters. This system was put to a severe test at the very outset of the war and confirmed its practicality. During the threatening period, due to the precise work of the headquarters' bodies, all the naval forces in a short period of time were shifted to the highest level of combat readiness and the surprise attack by Nazi aircraft during the first hours of war did not achieve its aim as the ships and naval bases fully maintained their fighting efficiency.

During the entire Great Patriotic War, the basic burden of fighting the Nazi invaders rested on the ground forces. The other armed services, including the Navy, directed their efforts toward the greatest possible support for the success of their combat operations. In this context the forces of the operational fleets and naval flotillas had to simultaneously carry out two main tasks: assist the troops in both defense and offense and fight against the enemy at sea.

In both defensive and offensive operations, naval forces reliably supported the strategic flanks of the Soviet Army; with naval gunfire and the landing of amphibious forces they effectively assisted the fronts and armies in defeating enemy forces in the coastal areas.

Intense struggle for strategic initiative was a major feature of combat during the war. Surprise attack gave the aggressor a significant advantage in the conduct of military operations early in the war. The Soviet Supreme High Command took every measure to alter the unfavorable course of combat, to achieve a turning point, and to establish prerequisites for the decisive rout of the interventionists.

The unprecedented steadfastness and stubbornness of the Soviet Armed Forces during the active strategic defensive undercut the strategic plans of the Wehrmacht Supreme Command and even the initial period of the war showed that the Nazi military adventure was doomed to defeat. During the most difficult times for the Soviet state, the powerful battle formations of our fleets turned all their fire power against the enemy and bolstered the flanks of the troops in coastal areas. During the initial period of the war, the Navy sent 400,000 officers, petty officers and sailors to the land fronts. Naval infantry brigades, naval rifle brigades, individual regiments and battalions organized from seamen were used in the most crucial areas of combat.

In defending the naval bases, the operational situation led to organizing a new form of joint operations among units and formations of the fleet, ground forces, and aviation under unified leadership; these were the defensive areas (Odessa, Sevastopol, Novorossiysk and others). This ensured centralized control and command over the diverse forces and closer cooperation between them. Later (from 1943) naval defensive areas (MOR) were organized and these included several naval bases. In 1945, the Navy included 13 such forces.

In the course of operations in the maritime sectors, the Navy provided the most effective aid to the troops in defeating the enemy forces by landing amphibious forces. As a total during the war years, over 100 amphibious forces were landed numbering more than 250,000 men with combat equipment and weapons; this was the equivalent of approximately 30 rifle divisions. The river flotillas alone, operating in direct operational-tactical cooperation with the field forces, formations, and units of the Red Army, landed 55 forces in the enemy flank and rear. Participating in the landing operations was a total of up to 2,000 ships and launches, around several thousand vessels, and about 10,000 aircraft. At the same time the Navy, by plans of active operations, did not allow the Nazi troops to carry out one major landing, although they already had experience in landing significant numbers of forces in the Western European theater of war.

Naval warfare included disrupting and thwarting enemy sea movements, attacking enemy ports and naval bases, laying active minefields, and supporting our own troop and economic goods shipments. In conducting combat operations at sea, great attention was given to winning air supremacy and to organizing a secure air defense for the ships at sea and in base.

In the struggle on the enemy lines of communications aviation and submarines were the main attack force. This assumed a more planned nature from the second half of 1943, when naval aviation, which during the first period of the war operated basically against the ground enemy, again began to carry out its immediate mission and the fleets received a significant number of new torpedo and ground-attack aircraft. By this time, the methods of employing the submarines had become more effective. While in 1941–1943, as a rule, they operated singly, for attacking convoys they were employed subsequently in operational-level coordination with aircraft and torpedo boats.

The methods of employing naval aviation were also improved: from attacks in small groups they shifted to massed attacks by mixed groups of torpedo planes, bombers and ground-attack aircraft. The depth of its operations reached 350–400 km.

The combined use of diverse naval forces significantly increased the effectiveness of combat operations on the enemy sea lines of communications. Having destroyed a total of around 1,400 ships with troops, ammunition, fuel, combat equipment and other cargo, our Navy provided much aid to the troops fighting on the Soviet-German Front.

The Navy also gained great experience in organizing the defense of its sea lines of communications. For our navigation the basic danger was the operations of enemy aviation and submarines, and in the Baltic, the use of mines. For this reason great attention was given to the questions of air, anti-submarine and anti-mine defense of the convoys and shipping areas. The defense of the sea lanes was organized chiefly within the daily combat activity of the fleet. The movement of convoys was supported, as a rule, by the men and weapons of special air defense areas deployed along the most important routes of the sea lanes. Fighters employed the direct cover method for the convoys (air patrolling) and with the development of radar, airfield alert close-in protection for the transports was organized in such a manner as to protect them against diverse enemy forces and to provide them pilotage behind sweeps.

The effective activities of the naval forces to protect our shipments are eloquently seen from the following facts: a total of 17 million tons of diverse cargo was transported over overseas lines of communications and more than 17 million tons via inland waterways.

The combat operations of naval forces against the ships of the Nazi coalition comprised a significant portion of naval warfare during the Great Patriotic War. A total of more than 1,300 enemy ships of different classes were sunk. Naval pilots downed in air combat and destroyed at airfields some 5,500 aircraft. On the Barents, Baltic, and Black Seas, the Navy bolstered the ground troops' flanks and their successful operations in the coastal sectors.

The increased use of naval forces in joint operations with troops brought about a change in the system of planning and organizing their actions. While in 1941–1942, they were employed in front and army operations, from 1944, as a rule, they were employed in strategic operations. For example, in the Crimean Operation, in addition to assisting the troops of the Fourth Ukrainian Front and the Detached Maritime Army, the Black Sea Fleet carried out the independent mission of stopping enemy communications between the Crimea and Romania and blockading the enemy troops in Sevastopol. In the Iasi-Kishinev Operation, simultaneously with direct support to the troops of the Third Ukrainian Front, the fleet made massed attacks against enemy ships and transports in Constanta and Sulina.

Leadership of the Navy was provided by the People's Commissariat of the Navy through the Main Navy Staff as well as the main and central directorates. Operational and strategic activities of the People's Commissariat of the Navy were determined by the nature of the missions confronting the fleets and naval flotillas which, up to 1984, in operational terms were under the commanders of the fronts (armies) for more effectively utilizing the forces in joint operations in the maritime sectors. The People's Commissariat of the Navy and the Main Naval Staff provided direct leadership (upon instructions from Headquarters) of the independent combat operations of the naval forces in the sea theaters and carried out the missions of developing the fleets and naval flotillas and their logistic support. After the fleets were put fully under the command of the People's Commissar of the

Navy, who at the same time became the Commander-in-Chief of the Navy, in the spring of 1944, a large portion of the questions concerning the planning and fleet operations began to be taken up by the People's Commissariat of the Navy and the Main Naval Staff.

Close, uninterrupted and dependable command of the forces was one of the main factors in achieving victory. As a rule, where this was organized on scientifically sound operational and tactical calculations, the course of events was anticipated and specific missions were assigned and success always followed.

A matter of constant concern for the commanders and staffs at all levels was the careful monitoring of the situation, the prompt and quick response to any change in it, defining and assigning new missions for conducting combat operations and supervising the carrying out of the issued orders and instructions. Field visits by representatives of the People's Commissariat of the Navy, the Main Naval Staff, the staffs of the fleets and flotillas made it possible to take measures promptly to eliminate arising difficulties, to ascertain the nature and scope of the help needed, to know in detail the actual degree of combat readiness of the men and the way issued orders and instructions were carried out and to effectively resolve the problems of cooperation among the diverse naval forces and the units, formations and field forces of the other Armed Services.

"The victory in the Great Patriotic War," pointed out the Decree of the CPSU Central Committee, "On the 40th Anniversary of the Victory of the Soviet People in the Great Patriotic War of 1941–1945, . . . has shown the superiority of Soviet military science and military art, the high level of strategic leadership and combat skill of our military personnel."[1]

During the years of the Great Patriotic War, the talent of such major naval figures as N. Kuznetsov, I. Isakov, A. Golovko, F. Oktyabr'skiy, I. Yumashev, V. Tributs, L. Vladimirskiy, Yu. Panteleyev, Yu. Rall, N. Basistyy, S. Zhavoronkov, M. Samokhin, N. Ostryakov, V. Yermachenkov, Ye. Preobrazhenskiy and many others became fully apparent. They made a great personal contribution to the defeat of the enemy and to the development of the Soviet naval art.

---

1. *Pravda*, 17 June 1984.

The force of Soviet Navymen augmented the Communist Party's constant concern and leadership of the Navy. The political indoctrination of all the commanding officers and political workers, the political bodies and party and Komsomol organizations was directed at increasing the morale of navy personnel. Heading this work were such experienced political workers as I. Rogov, N. Smirnov, A. Nikolayev, N. Kulakov, I. Azarov and S. Zakharov. By their personal example of courage and valor, wholehearted service to the motherland and the impassioned word of the propagandist, the communists and Komsomol members brought the will of the Party to all the fighting men, strengthened their certainty in overcoming all difficulties on the road to victory, and inspired them to heroic deeds.

In examining events of 40 years ago and in comparing the combat capabilities of the naval forces of those times and today, the question naturally arises: has the previous experience of the combat employment of the fleets lost its importance in the present stage of development of the Navy and naval theory? The question is a legitimate one as the physical plant or material base which determines the forms and methods of armed combat over this period has undergone fundamental qualitative changes. Nevertheless, there can only be one answer: no, it has not.

The combat experience was diverse and acquired in operations and battles that were grandiose in scope and unprecedented in fierceness and tenacity extending into all spheres of armed combat: on land, at sea, under water and in the air. It so touched all aspects of naval activities that its influence on the organizational development of the fleet, the development of naval theory, military training and indoctrination of the personnel and operational and combat training will be felt for a long time to come. However, this does not mean that in now solving new problems related to the development of the fleets and their employment, in the event the imperialist aggressors start a war, we must follow the same paths which led previously to the necessary result or seek out and choose those analogies which could be employed with modern weapons systems and combat equipment. Such an approach to the use of the experience of the last war is completely wrong and dangerous for the matter at hand, as the existing material base of armed combat at sea differs fundamentally from that used in the fight against the Nazi invaders.

"I have looked to the past," said V.I. Lenin, "only from the viewpoint of what is needed tomorrow and the day after for our policy."[2] These words of his should be the guiding principle in studying various topics of naval history.

The Great Patriotic War showed that the leading patterns in the development of military affairs are the growing organic relationship of policy and strategy, the obliterating of the distinction between the theater of military operations and the rear, the joint conduct of armed conflict by nations of coalitions, the increased dependence of the combat might of the armed forces upon the economy and scientific-technical progress, the high morale and ideological, psychological qualities of the Army and Navy personnel.

These patterns should be taken into account fully by us in developing the naval forces and in the navy's daily activities, for the threat of unleashing a new world war by the imperialists is now greater than ever before. In ignoring the lessons of history, the reactionary circles of the West, and primarily the United States, have declared a new "crusade" against socialism, and are endeavoring to achieve military supremacy over the socialist commonwealth nations. The deployment of first-strike missiles on the territory of a number of Western European countries, the increased military preparations of the United States in the Far East and the growing militarization of Japan are fraught with great danger.

"We cannot help but see the growing aggressiveness of imperialism and its attempts to achieve military supremacy over the socialist commonwealth," as was pointed out at a session of the Politburo of the CPSU Central Committee in October 1984. "Our nation does not intend to attack anyone. This is clear to any sensible person. But we will strengthen our defense capability, protecting the peaceful labor of the Soviet people and defending the cause of peace throughout the world."

In solving the fundamental problems of military-organizational development considering the experience of the Great Patriotic War, the Communist Party and the Soviet government have designated the main tasks in the military-technical area to be: achieving a close alliance of science with production in the interests of developing the most effective weapons models; a rational improvement in diverse combat equipment

---

2. V. I. Lenin, PSS [Complete Collected Works], Vol. 38, p. 136.

and weapons in accord with the growing demands of modern warfare; a transition to full automation of command and control of troops and weapons systems.

A scientifically sound and planned solution to the problems of military organizational development have made it possible for the Soviet Union during the post-war years to establish a balanced Navy consisting of nuclear submarines, surface vessels, missile-carrying and ASW naval aviation, naval infantry and coastal missile-artillery troops. That is, we have now been able to do what we could not do by 1941, that is, establish an ocean-going fleet capable of making powerful attacks against the ground installations and distributions of an aggressor's naval forces operating in any regions of the world's ocean.

With the development of the Navy, inevitably there will be changes in its missions, the forms and methods of the strategic and operational employment of the forces, the tactical procedures of their actions and the employment of weapons. The building up of the fleet and the development of the naval art in essence comprise a single process. In line with the fundamental change in the material base during the postwar years, such categories of military and naval art as cooperation, surprise, the massing of forces, attack, combat, maneuver, the pace of combat operations, combat readiness, and so forth have assumed a qualitatively new content.

The cooperation of the Armed Services branches, the branches of the army and naval forces, has been and remains a major principle of Soviet military and naval art. Its skillful realization is one of the main conditions for carrying out combat missions in modern armed combat at sea. The most advantageous combination of the combat capabilities of the diverse naval forces is presently the main demand in organizing combat operations at different levels.

Surprise attacks by the Soviet Army played an important role in the defeat of the Nazi invaders. An unexpected powerful attack against the Nazi troops made it possible to disrupt the plans of their command, to catch the enemy by surprise, to cause him the greatest losses, to seize the initiative and establish the necessary prerequisites for the further development of success.

Surprise, as a category of the military art, has maintained its importance at present. The United States and its NATO allies, in strengthening their arsenal of weapons, are focusing their attention primarily on first-strike weapons which are based upon ballistic missiles and cruise missiles. As the experience of local wars has shown, all the aggressors have planned on a surprise attack against their victims. This was achieved by the integrated use of diverse forces, a diverse arsenal of means and methods of reconnaissance, camouflage, ECM, and in certain instances the use of high-precision conventional weapons with great destructive force.

During these local wars there has been a tendency to bring together reconnaissance, attack and support resources into automated and rigidly correlated reconnaissance systems which make it possible to fight according to a new principle: "detect-blind-destroy." The United States has worked out several such mission-specialized systems. In the near future they will be part of the arms inventory. The aim of developing such systems has been to increase the arsenal of first-strike weapons.

The perfidy of the aggressors is well known. For this reason, it is essential to carefully study the methods by which they achieve surprise in order to be able to promptly detect the plans of the probable enemy and immediately localize all his attempts to make a surprise attack.

In the postwar years, the fact has become more and more apparent that ships with more advanced weapons and combat equipment are assuming an all-purpose nature and are capable of carrying out diverse missions. This has led to a situation where the forces of the Navy can carry out missions now which previously belonged only to other branches of the Armed Services. The spatial scope of armed combat at sea is acquiring a global all-spheres nature. The criterion of its scope characterized by the number of combat units or weapons carriers is being replaced by the criterion of the total power of the potential combat capabilities of the men and weapons. The increased spatial scope has, in turn, predetermined the ever increasing involvement of the other branches of the Service in combat operations.

The increased might of naval weapons during the war years gave a completely new content to such a category of naval art as attack. While previously an attack was an element of combat, during the Great Patriotic War in a number of instances this assumed operational dimensions. At present, in line with the equipping of the navies of foreign sea powers with long-range, high-precision weapons, the attack has become the dominant form for employing forces. It can achieve not only tactical but also operational and strategic goals.

The content of the main form of carrying out tactical mission, the sea battle, has also changed substantially. Its evolution during the war years was brought about by an increase in the distances of the clashes and their spatial scope with the change of these, in turn, being caused by the increased range of naval weapons, maneuverability, the cruising (flight) range of the weapons carriers, and by the involvement in combat of other branches of forces, primarily aviation. As a result of the increased range of naval weapons a new variety of combat has appeared—"non-contact," that is, beyond the visible range of the antagonists.

"Non-contact" and speed of combat will, obviously, be among the basic features of modern naval combat. There are very substantial prerequisites for this. Western specialists have pointed out that the American air and space systems are now capable in a short period of time, and with high reliability, to reveal the situation over enormous expanses of the world's oceans and contiguous territory and immediately relay data about it to the users, that is, create all prerequisites for employing the weapons immediately upon detecting the targets which are still hundreds of kilometers away from the strike forces.

This has become possible due to the extensive use of electronics which even during the war years had become a factor which largely determined military superiority over the enemy. Its penetration into all spheres of naval operations, particularly into the control systems of the forces, weapons, and combat equipment, has made it possible to rapidly collect various data on the situation, to analyze them, to give target designations, the current coordinates of targets, and make optimum decisions to carry out combat operations.

All the profound qualitative changes in the forms, methods, and procedures of armed combat at sea, as well as in its material base, have become possible due to the fact that Soviet military science, by analyzing war experience, has correctly established new patterns and incipient trends in the employment of naval forces brought about by the realization of recent scientific and technical accomplishments in combat experience. Only a scientific approach to an examination of the past helps in assessing its importance for the future reliably and objectively.

At a certain stage ongoing improvement in weapons systems and combat equipment will inevitably lead to a reassessment of the role or another branch of forces or class of ships. For this reason an important mission for command and scientific cadres is to promptly determine the occurrence of a qualitative shift in the development of the material base, to bring the concepts of the naval art into conformity with it and find new forms, methods and means of employing naval forces.

The unrestrained increase in the weapons arsenal of the NATO countries headed by the United States, the ignoring by their governments of the demands of the world community to check the arms race and direct the foreign policy of the Western powers toward a lessening of international tension are reminiscent of the aggressive aspirations of the Nazi leadership of Germany for world domination prior to World War II. This necessitates a high degree of vigilance and combat readiness on the part of all the naval forces. The older generation of Soviet people is well aware of where their reduction can lead. The combat readiness of the naval forces should always be such that under any conditions they can quickly shift to a war footing, enter the war in an organized manner, and successfully carry out assigned missions.

As long as military and political tension exists, as long as a nuclear missile danger from the aggressive imperialist forces hangs over our nation, as the CPSU Central Committee and Soviet government have pointed out, it is essential to keep our powder dry and to always be on guard to prevent a repetition of June 1941.

Even a cursory analysis of combat experience convinces one of its enormous importance for our fleet which is undergoing fundamental and complete transformation brought about by the scientific and technical revolution. Study and utilization of this experience in fleet construction and in forecasting its development protect us against the errors of a narrow practical approach, subjectivism, and rash schemes, and make it possible to draw correct conclusions from an analysis of our own military experience and the military practice of the imperialist navies. All of this is of exceptionally important significance for strengthening the defense capability of our nation and its sea power.

At present, the Soviet Navy possesses complex weapons systems and the latest varied combat hardware each of which, individually and together, introduces changes in the conditions of armed combat at sea. It is essential to disclose the new patterns and their specific influence on the use of all the branches of the armed forces in independent and joint operations with the other armed services, since the full realization of all the combat capabilities of the various forces in the best combination remains the most important requirement in organizing combat operations of any scale.

The results obtained from studying the combat experience of the Navy in the last war must be more widely employed in actual operational and combat training, for this experience serves as an inexhaustible source of knowledge essential for developing military-theoretical thinking, for the organizational development of our Navy and its strategic and operational use in a modern war, if the imperialist aggressors start it.

NOTES

Introduction

1. Bradford Dismukes and James McConnell, eds., *Soviet Naval Diplomacy* (New York: Pergamon Press, 1979), 16.
2. For an interesting article on the Anglo-American school of naval thought and its various challengers, see Martin Murphy and Toshi Yoshihara, "Fighting the Naval Hegemon," *US Naval War College Review* 68, no. 3 (2015), pp. 13–39.
3. Quoted in Sergei Chernyavskii, "The Era of Gorshkov: Triumph and Contradictions," *Journal of Strategic Studies* 28, no. 2 (2007), p. 285.
4. Ibid., p. 289.
5. David Winker, *Cold War at Sea* (Annapolis: Naval Institute Press, 2000), 51.
6. Dominik G. Nargele, "The Soviet Naval Infantry," in L. Bartlett Merrill, ed., *Assault from the Sea: Essays on the History of Amphibious Warfare* (Annapolis: Naval Institute Press, 1983).
7. Donald Chipman, "Admiral Gorshkov and the Soviet Navy," *Air University Review* 33, no. 5 (1982), pp. 28–47.
8. Sergei Gorshkov, *The Sea Power of the State* (Annapolis: Naval Institute Press, 1979), ix.
9. Winker, *Cold War at Sea*, 10.
10. Gorshkov, *The Sea Power of the State*, 59.
11. Ibid., 159.
12. Ibid., 249.
13. Ibid., 251–252.
14. George H. Miller, "'Commentary' following Sergei G. Gorshkov, 'Navies in War and Peace,'" U.S. Naval Institute *Proceedings* 100, no. 1 (1974), p. 27.
15. John Hibbits, "Admiral Gorshkov's Writings: Twenty Years of Naval Thought," in Paul Murphy, ed., *Naval Power in Soviet Policy* (Washington, DC: US Air Force, 1978), 2.

Chapter Two. Ethos

1. Colin Gray, "Strategic Thoughts for Defence Planners," *Survival* 52, no. 3 (2010), p. 160.

Chapter Three. Science

1. S. G. Gorshkov, *The Sea Power of the State* (Annapolis: Naval Institute Press, 1979), 275.
2. B. Dismukes and J. McConnell, eds., *Soviet Naval Diplomacy* (New York: Pergamon Press, 1979), 38.

Chapter Four. Art

1. For a fuller analysis of Nimitz's "calculated risk," see: Robert Rubel, "Deconstructing Nimitz's Principle of Calculated Risk," *U.S. Naval War College Review* 68, no. 1 (2015), pp. 31–45.

ABOUT THE EDITOR

Kevin Rowlands is a commander in the Royal Navy and has served in various ships and shore-based staffs. He holds master's degrees in defense studies and education and a PhD in war studies from King's College London. He has published numerous articles and is the book reviews editor of the UK's *Naval Review*.